# Newshounds

## HOLIDAY CLUB RESOURCE MATERIAL

Peter Graystone

A complete five-day holiday club programme for 5–11s
An introduction to the life, death and resurrection of Jesus
Leaders' notes for preparation, presentation of the Good News, and activities
Five daily newspapers with news, Bible stories and activities
Drama scripts and craft ideas
An all-age 'family service' outline

## WITH ACCOMPANYING VIDEO

Scripture Union
130 City Road
London EC1V 2NJ

## THANKS TO...

*Newshounds* is dedicated to Celia Morgan who has continually encouraged me to work at the creative and innovative edge of children's ministry and who has been good news to countless children.

The scheme was developed between 1992 and 1993 at the Scripture Union holiday for children at Tockington, near Bristol, England. Many thanks to the talented team.

Unless otherwise specified, Scripture quotations in this publication are from the International Children's Bible, New Century Version (Anglicised Edition) copyright © 1991 by Word (UK) Ltd, Milton Keynes, England. Used by permission.

Cover design by Tony Cantale Graphics
Design and illustration by Tony Cantale Graphics

**British Library Cataloguing-in-Publication Data**
A catalogue record for this book is available from the British Library.

Printed and bound in Great Britain by
Ebenezer Baylis & Son Ltd, The Trinity Press,
Worcester and London.

# CONTENTS

• **PLUS** five daily newspapers to pull out from the centre


## STOP PRESS!!!
### EXTRA RESOURCE!
*Newshounds* **cassette** featuring the *Newshounds* song,
plus a variety of other songs.

Available from Scripture Union Mail Order, 9–11 Clothier Road,
Bristol BS4 5RL; tel. 0117–9719709. Price £6.95.
(Trade orders direct to Plankton Records, 236 Sebert Road,
Forest Gate, London E7 0NP; tel. 0181 534 8500.
Catalogue no. of tape PCN 145.)

# Introduction

**N**EWSHOUNDS is a five-day holiday club package for 5–11 year-olds, followed by a church service which is appropriate for all ages. Because it is a basic introduction to the life and teaching of Jesus, it is suitable for children who have little or no knowledge of the Bible; but it should also appeal to children who have Christian grown-ups at home. Alongside each other, both churched and unchurched children will increase their understanding of who Jesus was, what he said and did, why he died, and why he was raised from the dead.

**T**HERE are two splendid anachronisms at the heart of the programme. The first is the impossible supposition that there were daily newspapers at the time of Jesus' earthly life, which could have recorded his activities. It is these newspapers – which you will find ready to pull out, photocopy and use in the centre of the book – that are the appealing core of the club for children. On the outside the newspapers contain information about Jesus, things to talk about in small groups, suggestions for prayer, puzzles based on Bible stories and so on. The inside pages of the newspapers are supplied blank. These should carry local news, photographs of the club, the weather forecast, jokes, questions and articles supplied by the children, and so on. The inside pages are compiled by the leaders of the club during the evening, photocopied and distributed the next day (full instructions for doing this are supplied in the book).

**T**HE second anachronism is the idea that a television studio could have broadcast information about the life of Jesus. The scripts for each day tell the story of two media workers whose lives are profoundly affected by finding out about him. They are a point of reference for the children to discover what difference following Jesus might make to them in the twentieth century. The news broadcasts that the media workers supposedly make are available on the *Newshounds–Location Report* video, which you can obtain wherever you bought this book. But it is also possible to use the programme without the video, by setting up a mock TV studio in the room and performing a version of the 'broadcasts' live. Scripts for this are contained in the book, but please note that, while covering the same subject matter, they are not identical to those in the video.

**T**HE format of *Newshounds* is very varied. It has moments of fast-moving slapstick, but also quieter and more thoughtful stretches. Some of the programme is presented to the children from the front in the form of imaginative Bible teaching, music, drama and participation. Other parts take place in small groups, with children developing relationships with particular leaders as they talk, enjoy the newspapers and play together. There are optional craft activities for these small-group times as well.

**N**EWSHOUNDS may be used on five consecutive mornings during school holidays or half-terms, but an alternative set of timings is given so that it may be adapted for use in term time or perhaps one evening a week for five weeks.

<5>

# Running Newshounds

<6>

**The following Countdown may be adapted to suit your church**

## 10 months before the event

Make the decision to run a holiday club and confirm the dates with your own and other local church leaders. Book the hall where it will take place, checking its safety and your public liability insurance requirements.

## 8 months before

Announce to the congregation that the holiday club will take place. Set in motion the means of financing it.

## 6 months before

Write to individuals in the church who have potential to be presenters, group leaders, newspaper editors, photographers, actors, musicians, aerobics instructors, administrators or refreshment makers. Invite them to join the team.

## 3 months before

Buy a copy of *Newshounds* for each member of the team and the *Newshounds–Location Report* video. Try to identify what skills need to be developed in the team and plan how you can provide them with training in order to maximise the impact of the time they have with the children. Scripture Union's Do-It-Yourself training pack, *Working with Children*, may help you. (Price £18.34, including postage, from **Scripture Union Training Unit, 26–30 Heathcoat Street, Nottingham NG1 3AA.**)

## 2 months before

Gather the leaders together to begin making detailed plans. Familiarise yourselves with the material, hold any training that has seemed desirable, make a list of the resources that are needed, allocate preparation tasks to particular people, and pray together.

Write to the Christian Publicity Organisation, Garcia Estate, Canterbury Road, Worthing, West Sussex, BN13 1BW to find out what publicity material is available.

## 1 month before

Remind the children in the church and their parents that *Newshounds* will take place. Invite them to book the dates and times in their diaries, if they have not already done so. Make arrangements for hiring or borrowing any technical or electronic equipment that is required.

## 2 weeks before

Advertise the event beyond the local congregation. Put up posters and distribute leaflets through front doors or in schools if permission is given. Because of the theme of the club, local newspapers and free-sheets may be more interested than usual in carrying details of the event (see the section on publicity).

## At least 1 week before

Meet with the leaders to pray and discuss any last minute requirements. Gather together all the resources that are needed. Record any music that is required and the 'eyewitness' interviews which will be needed if the video is not being used. Prepare the visual aids. Musicians and actors should have rehearsed and learnt their parts by now. Small group leaders should be familiarising themselves thoroughly with the Bible and discussion content of the *Newshounds* newspaper.

## 1 day before

Move into the hall, prepare the furniture and displays, set out as much equipment as possible. Prepare the inside pages of the first edition of *The Daily Hound*, and photocopy enough for every child to have one. Only leave when the hall is ready to receive the first child.

## 1 hour before

The entire team should arrive for Bible study and prayer.

## SETTING

The holiday club is set in and around a news studio. The basic anachronism of the scheme (which will be accepted with delight by children but may be queried by less imaginative adults) is that the events in Jesus' life are taking place somewhere in the area and are being reported on a television broadcast. A serial drama runs from day to day, including two TV journalists whose broadcasts explain what happened to Jesus and consider who he is. Their reports are available on the *Newshounds–Location Report* video, for showing to the children each day. However, if a video and television is not available, a simplified version can be created live in the hall itself using two actors and a pre-recorded voice (scripts are given in this book).

In this make-believe setting, the reporters in the newsroom also produce a daily newspaper (the logic of this does not bear too much analysis either, but this does not spoil the children's enjoyment). *The Daily Hound* is published each day and each child gets a copy. This will be a highlight of their day and they will almost certainly want to collect the newspapers. Whilst part of the session is spent watching the presentation at the front of the room, the time that counts most in terms of quality is that spent in a small group enjoying the newspaper. The fact that the most enjoyable part of the morning is also the time when Bible teaching and prayer take place explicitly is one of the hidden advantages of *Newshounds*.

The illustration on page 7 shows how a reasonably sized hall can be laid out for up to a hundred children (a larger number of children would require more space). There are basically three areas.

## Presentation area

This is the site of the video and screens, the 'studio' acting area, the chat-show testimonies, the game show, the musicians, and anything else which is part of the presentation. Children should be made aware that this end of the hall, which may contain a lot of expensive, even dangerous, equipment is for leaders only.

If you are showing videos to a fairly large number of people, you might like to use a video projector onto a large screen or a number of monitors or television sets spread around the audience. The first way works well and modern LCD video projectors are easy to set up, but they do need effective blackout and they are expensive to hire. If you opt for the multi-set showing, it is important to understand the difference between monitors and televisions to establish what connections and sockets they will need, and how much cable you will need to run round all the sets in such a way that people will not trip over them. The sets must be mounted on sturdy, safe stands high enough for everyone to see them

clearly. Contact a specialist video equipment supplier in the *Yellow Pages* for information about how to set up this kind of viewing.

## Central seating area

The centre is a space (not with chairs, but perhaps with mats on the floor) in which children sit for all activities that are presented from the front and involve everyone.

## Perimeter

Around the edge of the hall are small areas marked out with chairs. (These may not be sat on, since groups often feel more comfortable on the floor, but they do define a particular area of the hall as a recognisable base for each child.) Each area is given a wacky name after a breed of dog and has a particular group leader attached to it. Activities for small groups take place here, and this is the point at which *The Daily Hound* is given out and used each day. Children move from this area to the centre and back several times during the session.

It is Scripture Union's earnest recommendation that churches should try to achieve a ratio of at least one adult to every four children. They consist of the following people, although in some cases team members will play more than one role:

### Vital

- An overall coordinator
- Actor/presenters – Link man or woman, Producer

If the *Newshounds–Location Report* video is not being used, two further actors playing Jake Newshound (the broadcaster) and Anne O'Pinion (the religious affairs commentator), with other voices on pre-recorded audio-tape, are also needed to perform 'live broadcasts' covering the same incidents in Jesus' life.

- DJ to front *The Really Kicking Hound Show*, leading songs and prayers
- Other musicians

<7>

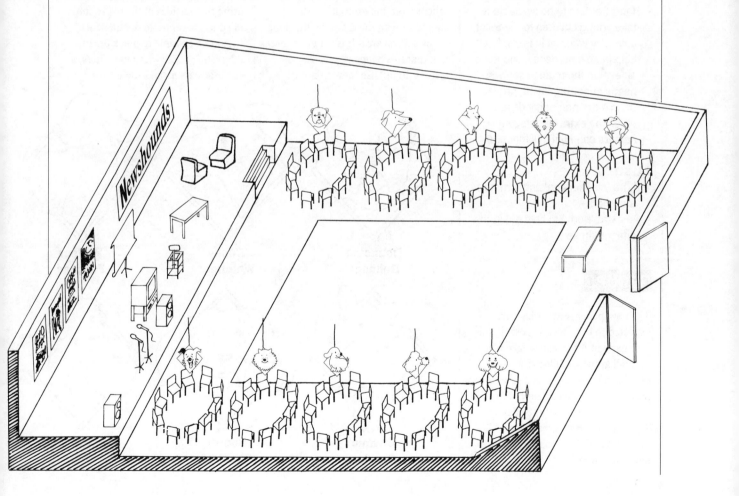

- Sports correspondent to lead the *Aerobihound work-out*
- Game-show host to run the daily game *Gladihound*
- Chat-show host to interview people on *Houndaround*
- Guest celebrities to be interviewed on *Houndaround*, a different celebrity each day
- One leader for each small group of eight children
- At least two people to welcome and register children
- Editor/compiler of *The Daily Hound*
- Photographer
- Resource and technical equipment coordinator if you are using video
- A First Aider

## Desirable
- An extra leader for every small group
- Extra help with producing, photocopying and folding *The Daily Hound*
- Security – someone to patrol outside the hall
- Refreshment coordinator, for both children and the team
- Hand-holders to be available to take young children to the toilet, calm any who are in tears, fetch help in an emergency, and keep an eye on the team to see who needs encouragement, prayer, or an extra pair of hands at any time. The extra leaders and helpers can fulfil this function.

## Luxury
- Extra 'cleaners up' and furniture arrangers
- An extra 'body' to help out in the difficult times

<8>

## GROUPS

The newspaper times, which are expected to become the most significant parts of *Newshounds*, take place in small groups. Children are allocated to a particular group as soon as they arrive for the first time, and they stay with that group day by day. There are separate groups for 5–7 year-olds and 8–11 year-olds (if you have the numbers, it would be worth splitting the older age group into 8–9s and 10–11s), and the newspaper contains different activities for older and younger children. Good friends should be kept together. Pastoral sensitivity should overrule strict adherence to the age-groups if two friends or brothers and sisters feel a strong urge to stay together despite being on different sides of the age divide. An ideal number for a small group is six to eight but if two leaders are available for each group it may be possible to accommodate twelve or fourteen.

The groups should be given fun names after different types of dog, and there should be a sign above each circle of chairs indicating the name (some examples are given in the illustration). The chief function of the group leader is to befriend each child in his or her group: this is more important than any individual activity. During group events, the leader should give instructions and encouragement, provide materials, pray with children and try to engage them in conversation – both formally about the subjects suggested in *The Daily Hound* and informally about the children's lives and likes. During presentations from the front, he or she should sit with the group on the floor of the central area. It is very important that this happens, and that the leaders do not use these times to clear away left-over materials or chat idly to other workers.

At the end of the club each child should know his or her own leader better than any other adult in the room, and group leaders should know enough about the children in their care to be able to tell others the best way to pray about each one.

## PUBLICITY

Posters and leaflets specially designed for this club are available from the **Christian Publicity Organisation, Garcia Estate, Canterbury Road, Worthing, West Sussex BN13 1BW**. They can be used among the children of the congregation and their friends, and in local schools.

However, the nature of this club may well be of special interest to local newspapers and free-sheets, which would allow you to spread information about the club wider than usual. About two weeks before the event, take some good quality black and white photographs of children at work compiling *The Daily Hound* (by using the outsides of the paper supplied in the centre of the book, it should be possible to mock up an interesting scene with typewriters, a camera, scissors and some happy

**Bouncing Bulldogs**

**Wacky Whippets**

**Perfect Puppies**

**Cosmic Corgies**

**Sporty Spaniels**

**Powerful Poodles**

children). Send them to the news editor of the paper with a press release (adapt the words in the sample below to include your own details). Do not be tempted to write more (it is the photo that the editor will mainly be interested in: if he wants to know more he will either contact you or send a reporter). In a covering note, name all the children in the photograph and give a telephone number at which you can be contacted. If you have a positive relationship with the local press already, telephone the news editor shortly after sending the material and offer more help if it would be useful.

### Sample Press Release
**A rival for (*the name of the local newspaper*)!**
Children at (*the name of your church*) enjoy (*the name of the local newspaper*), but they think they can do even better! They are turning into investigative journalists to write and edit their own newspaper *The Daily Hound* as part of the *Newshounds* holiday-club week. The club, which runs from Monday (*date*) to Friday (*date*) in (*the name of the road*), also features music, Bible stories and games. It is open to all 5–11 year-olds and the fun starts at (*time*). Look out! You could be on the front page!

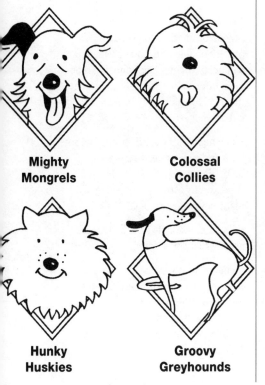

**Mighty Mongrels**

**Colossal Collies**

**Hunky Huskies**

**Groovy Greyhounds**

# The Daily Hound

One of the main features of the *Newshounds* concept is its daily newspaper. You will find the framework you require to create these newspapers on the six double-page spreads which you can pull out from the centre of the book. You will see that the outer pages of the *The Daily Hound* newspapers are created for you (on pages 27–31 and 34–38). (These contain a story from the Gospels presented in the form of a newspaper report, some questions for discussion in groups, and some puzzles.) The inner pages of the newspapers will consist of blank columns, and the template for these is at the centre of the book (pages 32–33). This template may be used again and again for every issue of *The Daily Hound*. Thus, to make up the newspapers: photocopy the double-page spread for the day's edition of the newspaper onto one side of an A3-size sheet of paper (you will need one for each child attending the holiday club), then photocopy the template onto the other side of the sheet to create the inner pages. Completed and photocopied daily for each child, the newspapers become a treasured part of the club.

The most effective way of using the newspapers is for the inner pages to be filled with topical news and entertainment features that are specific to the children and leaders who are present during the week. To give maximum value to the opportunity this presents, a home computer, word processor or typewriter should be used to create text that gives a convincing newspaper-type appearance. Photographs and drawings should be added. Using the 'instant art' graphics on pages 11 and 12 will also add that extra finish to your newspapers.

A less effective, but moderately engaging alternative would be to fill the centre pages with handwritten and hand-drawn contributions. It is self-evident that this is less satisfactory, but unlike the typed version it requires virtually no effort at all.

A third option, which is in every way less exciting but gives an option to those who simply cannot manage to create the newspapers, is to fold the A3 spread for the outer pages of the newspaper and photocopy it as an A4 double-sided sheet – the Bible passage on the front and the questions and puzzles on the reverse.

Assuming that the first or second options are taken, the key to the success of the paper is that children should have the prospect of finding in it their own names and the names of leaders and friends. One member of the leadership team should be appointed Editor and should be responsible for writing or compiling the text overnight so that the news children read the next day is topical. Some or all of the following items should be included.

### NEWS REPORTS
Incidents that occur during the club should be written about as if they were of urgent importance, in the style of a tabloid daily and mentioning as many people as possible. The question of what is newsworthy will vary from location to location, but even the most ordinary events can be appealing for children to read about if they recognise the context. Ideas for news stories include difficulties narrowly avoided, names of those who were first to arrive and last to leave, research into who has come the greatest distance and who the least, a child's unusual hobby, good wishes sent to children who are unwell, items of lost property, details of crafts that have been done, reviews of the *Newshounds–Location Report* video, the game show or the aerobics, requests for particular songs, a summary of 'the story so far' for those who have joined late and all the triv-

<9>

ial and not-so-trivial highlights and low-points of each day's programme. An example could be:

**Squash splosh disaster**

Three children were recovering last night after being drenched in a dangerous collision at the *Newshounds* holiday club. Leader Mrs Sally Windermere was carrying a large jug of orange squash from the kitchen to the front of the room when James McKenzie of the Bouncing Bulldogs ran backwards into her. Sally is reported to have yelled, jumped and emptied the contents of the jug over James and the Jones twins, Tabitha and Terry. Onlooker Martin Jakes said, 'I couldn't believe it. It was like a huge orange fountain. If I hadn't got out the way I'd have been soaked.' When asked whether Sally was cross, nine year-old Harriet Parker said, 'I think she was very patient, but I was furious since the squash went on the model I was making.' James McKenzie was heard to apologise before licking the orange off his knees…(and so on!)

<10>

## PHOTOGRAPHS

Children will enjoy seeing photographs of people they know in the same way that they will enjoy reading their names. The photos do not have to relate to the news items (although a picture of the after-effects of the drink spillage would obviously have been a good accompaniment to the article above). Photographs should be taken during the club and then developed at the nearest high street shop that will produce prints in an hour (or overnight if it is possible to leave it that late). Remembering that the photographs will be photocopied in black and white, the best results will come from black and white film, but most colour prints will give a reasonably good reproduction if they are crisply focused. If black and white film is being used, you need to be aware that most agencies cannot return them within an hour. You could use a film like Ilford XP2 monochrome film, which gives black and white prints but is developed using a standard colour process and so can be processed just as quickly as a colour film.

## NEWS OF CLUB EVENTS

Previews of the next day's events and any special attractions could be given in order to encourage day-by-day loyalty among the children. In particular, news about the all-age service could be given in this way. Some headlines and illustrations, which might help you make these eye-catching, are given on pages 11 and 12.

## WEATHER FORECAST

Information about this can be found on local television or radio and added to make the paper genuinely topical. Graphics to go with this report are given on page 12.

## JOKES

Invite children to submit these. (A postbox could be provided so that children have an easy way of submitting their favourite jokes; but encourage them to give jokes orally to the editor of the newspaper as well, so that those who cannot write their ideas down are not excluded.) Remember to print the name of the person who submitted the joke, perhaps in italics after each one. As soon as children begin to see their names attached to these, this element of the paper will be inundated with suggestions.

## AN AGONY AUNT

If a problem page is included, the questioners should be assured of anonymity. This may be a particularly useful method for children to find the answers to questions they have about what Christians do and believe.

## PROFILES OF LEADERS

A very popular item could be a questionnaire put to a particular leader, alongside a photograph of her or him. On the whole the questions should not be particularly serious. Some suggestions are:

What do you like best about *Newshounds*?
If you weren't at the *Newshounds* club, where in the world would you most like to be?
If you were an animal, what would you choose to be?
Who in the world would you most like to custard pie?
If there was a fire, what would you rush to grab and save?
What is your favourite band?
What is your favourite sport?
Who is the most famous person you have ever met?
If you had three wishes, what would they be?
What is the most daring thing you have ever done?

## CHILDREN'S QUESTIONS

An extension of the questionnaire above might involve children writing or asking questions about the leaders (perhaps using a postbox again); the answers to these could appear the next day.

## CHILDREN'S DRAWINGS

By inviting drawings as well as written contributions, children of all ages and intellectual stages are able to contribute and see their work valued.

## COMPETITIONS

Providing a caption to a cartoon, colouring a picture, writing a poem, solving a puzzle, making a good suggestion for the club, and so on.

Those who wish to use a word processor in order to give a really professional look to the newspapers will need to know the following technical information in order to match the inside pages to the design of the outside pages:

• The headlines have been set in 48pt bold and the subheadings in 15pt bold. The typeface used is Helvetica Bold, a sans serif font available in many software packages.

• The text size is 11pt. The typeface used is Plantin, a common serif font.

• The column widths are respectively 174mm single column layout, 84mm for a two column layout, and 54mm for a three column layout. The depth of the type columns on the page is 255mm.

<11>

**AUNT AGGIE**

**OVER YOU**

*Invitation*

"*Overheard!*"  "*Overheard!*"

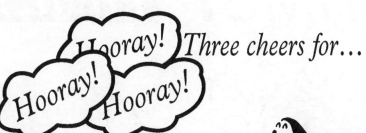

Hooray! *Three cheers for…*  Hooray! Hooray!

**NEWS**

Lost property

**NEWS**

**TIME TO…**

These instant art items are copyright free. You can use them to produce your own newspapers!

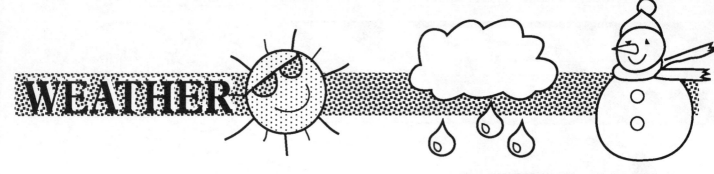

# WEATHER

Your Jokes Ha! Ha Ha

WEATHER FORECAST

? Competition ?

CROSSWORD

Recipes

MEET THE LEADER

Today's Programme

CuRioSItY cOrnEr ? ? ? ? ?

QUIZZZ ?TIME?

QUIZ TIME!

YOUR LETTERS

CRASH! BANG!

# The Programmes

## TIMETABLES

Times are given for both a morning and evening event

| AM | | PM | |
|---|---|---|---|
| 9.30 | or | 6.15 | Leaders arrive, prayer, last minute preparation |
| 10.15 | or | 6.30 | Opening credits – children are shown to groups |
| 10.30 | or | 6.45 | Headlines – an introduction and welcome |
| 10.35 | or | 6.50 | Studio dialogue – a serial drama |
| 10.40 | or | 6.55 | *Aerobihound* – a work out |
| 10.45 | or | 7.00 | *Newshounds–Location Report* video or *Good News at Ten* drama – Bible teaching , plus comment |
| 10.55 | or | 7.10 | *The Daily Hound* – the newspaper, discussion and prayer |
| 11.15 | or | 7.30 | *Gladihound* – a zany game involving everyone |
| 11.30 | or | 7.45 | *Houndaround* – a chat show format for testimonies |
| 11.40 | or | 7.55 | *The Really Kicking Hound Show* – praise and prayers |
| 11.55 | or | 8.10 | Studio dialogue – a serial drama |
| 12.00 | or | 8.15 | Closedown – children leave, leaders evaluation, preparation |
| 12.30 | or | 9.15 | Leaders leave |

Note that the children arrive from 10.15, but that the formal start is at 10.30, giving a 90-minute programme. Work with children of this age lasting two hours or more must be registered with the local authority under the Children Act of 1989. It is important to be aware of this if it is planned to extend the duration of the club with craft or games. Although there is no legal requirement to register a *Newshounds* club, you can only benefit from contacting the social services department for help and advice.

## LEADERS' PREPARATION

Each day the leaders need to focus their minds on the task ahead before the children arrive. The programmes begin with suggestions for Bible study and prayer at an adult level. If the club is run in the morning, this should take up most of the time allocated, with only a few minutes given to last-minute preparations that can-

not be done the day before. If the club takes place in the evening, this time is a shorter one with brief prayers (making allowance for people who have to leave work early in order to help run the event), and a longer time of Bible study takes place *after* the children have left, in anticipation of the following day's subject.

## OPENING CREDITS

As children arrive, they should be welcomed at the door. At least two people (more if there are large numbers of children, particularly on the first day) sit at a desk there. Their task is to record the name, telephone number and age of each child, to note any esential health or dietary requirements, and to decide which group to allocate children to. There are two categories of group: **Wee Hounds** (children aged 5-7) and **Hunky Hounds** (children aged 8-11). Some flexibility is needed here in order to keep good friends together, and siblings may have distinct preferences either for staying together or for keeping apart!

Since a large number of children need to be admitted in a short space of time, only a few details are needed at this stage and the registration form (see below) will give all the essential information. If there is an emergency, such as a fire, it is vital that the welcomers have this record of who is in the room. If a child has an accident, the telephone number will be needed urgently, so it is important that it is recorded at the door while young children have an adult with them to make sure it is correct. The same applies to special details such as health or dietary requirements. At this hectic time before the programme begins, anyone not leading a small group or registering children

<13>

---

**REGISTRATION FORM**

NAME

TELEPHONE

AGE

| ATTENDANCE | DAY 1 | DAY 2 | DAY 3 | DAY 4 | DAY 5 |
|---|---|---|---|---|---|

| CATEGORY | WEE HOUNDS | HUNKY HOUNDS |
|---|---|---|

Anything special the leaders should know?

**GROUP**

| | |
|---|---|
| Bouncing Bulldogs | Cosmic Corgis |
| Wacky Whippets | Sporty Spaniels |
| Perfect Puppies | Powerful Poodles |
| Mighty Mongrels | Hunky Huskies |
| Colossal Collies | Groovy Greyhounds |

Tick the relevant boxes

## RECORD CARD

Name

Age                    Birthday

Group

Home Address



Tel.

Parent's Names

Friend with whom you came

How did you hear about Newshounds?
(Which church, school, friend, etc?)



Other details (health, etc.)



should be standing by the door ready to take children to the group to which they have been allocated and introduce them by name to their group leader. While they are doing this, they should tell children where the toilets are, where to hang their coats and any other practical information.

Once the children have arrived at their small group, they are given a **press pass**. This is for them to wear, either with a safety pin or round the neck with a ribbon, in order to identify them. There is a different one for each day and children can collect them. Each day the pass requires them to contribute new information about themselves. In this way every child can be actively involved as soon as he or she arrives. The outline for the press pass can be found in each day's programme later in the book. It may be photocopied straight from the page or used as a prototype for a card which is specific to the local event.

While the children are occupied with this, the group leader should find out more information about them, which is recorded on a separate and more detailed record card (see above). This should be done in a friendly and relaxed way so that children gain confidence in the leader. Obviously the groups will grow larger during this time as more children arrive.

## HEADLINES

Everyone comes together for this activity and sits on the floor in the centre of the room. The leaders of the groups should tell children where to sit. This part of the programme should begin unannounced with the exciting jingle from the *Newshounds –Location Report* video being shown to create an atmosphere of joyful anticipation. This jingle occurs as a separate item before each episode on the video. If the video is not being used, buy or borrow from the local record library a cassette or CD of atmospheric jingles and play it at a substantial volume; or do the same with live music if you have musicians of suitable calibre. It should be followed immediately by the actor playing the link man/woman reading some imaginary news headlines, as if this were the beginning of a news programme. A script is given in each day's programme, but more fun can be had if the headlines are localised to refer to activities and personalities in the club itself, or to (appropriately innocuous) genuine news events of the day. This should be done formally with all the professionalism of a studio, almost as if the audience were not there but were watching at a distance on a television set. It is followed by a welcome from the overall coordinator of the event, done in a

racy style as if he or she was the continuity announcer of a professional television production.

## STUDIO DIALOGUES

These scripted pieces of dialogue follow without introduction after the Headlines. For almost all of them, the link man is seated at a desk, perhaps made to look a little like a broadcasting suite with a microphone and headphones. Sometimes he talks into the microphone, as if to the listening audience; sometimes to the producer, who stands beside him.

## AEROBIHOUND

Led by an enthusiastic and energetic leader, either male or female, these exercises should take place in the centre of the room to the accompaniment of a loud disco track with a clear rhythm. The music should be up-to-date and familiar to children from the mainstream pop chart, but check the suitability of the words! It is important that a tape deck with sufficiently powerful amplification to fill the hall is used. The movements should be simple, repetitive and not likely to strain muscles! Try to maintain the vague impression of the activity taking place in a studio and being broadcast on television; Breakfast TV often has this kind of feature. If in doubt, borrow a beginners' tape from a video library, remembering that children are not capable of so rigorous a routine as adults!

## GOOD NEWS AT TEN

At this point there are two alternatives in the programme. Those who are using the *Newshounds –Location Report* video should show the appropriate day's episode without further introduction. Each day the presenter, Jake Newshound, introduces news of an incident in Jesus' ministry, and interviews two eye-witnesses whose stories are illustrated by cartoon artwork. Then he talks to the religious affairs correspondent, Anne

<14>

O'Pinion, who comments on what has just been seen, draws conclusions about the nature of Jesus and faith in him, and poses some questions. There being no 'talks' in the traditional sense in the *Newshounds* programme, this is the central focus of the club's teaching about Christianity.

If the video is not being used, some of its content should be performed live in front of the children in *Good News at Ten*. This requires two further actors and a series of pre-recorded taped interviews. The actors playing Jake Newshound and Anne O'Pinion (who also appear on the video) sit behind a desk in the style of a newscaster and a religious affairs editor. Obviously the genders of the actors could be changed. Scripts for this are given each day. Jake Newshound's report could be read, but Anne O'Pinion's replies to the questions are not given verbatim so that they can be pitched at a level appropriate to the children who are attending the event each day. It is crucial that these replies should be thought through in great detail by the person taking this part. They are the most direct and serious expressions of Christian teaching during the club, even though they are presented in a very engaging way. Of course, it is also extremely important that they are kept brief and simple.

The eye-witness interview that comes in the middle should be heard but not seen. The same tape deck that played the aerobics music could be used. The interviewer on this audio sequence could be the person playing the part of Jake Newshound (although there is no reason why another person should not pre-record this section). A different leader each day should play the role of the eyewitness. For added impact others could add sound effects and crowd noises in the background when the recording is made.

A burst of brassy live music or an up-beat jingle from a commercially produced cassette or CD should be used to introduce and possibly conclude the whole *Good News at Ten* section. (Listen to the credit sequences from television news broadcasts to know what kind of introduction is suitable.)

## THE DAILY HOUND

At this point the children go back into their small groups around the edge of the room and their group leader distributes to every child a copy of the day's edition of the newspaper, *The Daily Hound*. This activity is one of the main focuses of the event since it gives children a chance to think through Christian issues, read the Bible, express their own point of view and pray about things that are of personal concern to them. All this will be taking place in the context of excitement at receiving the newspaper.

In each edition of *The Daily Hound* there are things for the group leader and children to talk about, and suggestions for ways of praying. The complexity of what is suggested rises through the week as children get used to taking part in these activities. The group leaders should treat the front and back pages of the paper as a child-level Bible study, even though it appears in a lively and unexpected form. The questions for discussion are given at two levels. It is anticipated that one set will be appropriate for Wee Hounds and the other for Hunky Hounds, but a leader may decide that the sophistication of the children she or he has lends itself better to the whole group using only one set of questions, so a certain amount of discretion should be used.

Follow the suggested questions and prayers if they are helpful, but do not be afraid to talk about something different if the children lead the conversation in that direction. Each time there will be some element of personal testimony from the leader to contribute to the discussion. Be ready for this – each leader's own unique story will be a very powerful contribution to the way God works in the children during the week. Respect the children's accounts of their experience too, even if they are unusual! Obviously the groups work best if the leaders are one step ahead of the children, so it is important that they have seen the text in advance, have read the story, and have a well-formed idea of what they will say and do.

You will notice that the children do not need Bibles and only need pencils if they choose to do the puzzle during this time. This has been done deliberately to help start the activity in a disciplined way: all you need is a circle of children sitting or sprawling on the floor. On the first day the leader should read the Bible story aloud with a good deal of expression to the children who can follow it in their own copies. On subsequent days it may be that some children in the older groups would enjoy reading it aloud, and that should be permitted, but it is extremely important that no child is expected to read if he or she does not ask to.

There is the possibility of a slight difficulty. It has been known that the newspaper becomes so popular that children want to read the inside pages first to see whether their names or photographs appear. Each leader has to deal with this in an appropriate way, either giving them a chance to read the rest and then insisting on attention, or making it clear that the outsides of the newspaper are to be looked at together first before children can enjoy the inside on their own.

Some groups will work better than others, and some days will go better than others. Leaders should not worry about this, just make the most of opportunities as they come. If the discussion is not working on a particular day, individual group leaders should feel free to abandon it and do the puzzle instead – that's what it's there for. If, on occasion, the suggestions for prayer are not working, the leader alone could say a short prayer and let that be sufficient. Although these activities occupy a space that might traditionally be called a 'quiet time', they do not have to be quiet or follow any traditional pattern. They are designed to show children that reading the Bible is a positive experience (no matter how one goes about it) and that prayer matters because we have everything to gain and nothing to lose by telling God what is on our minds.

It is important to finish this part of the programme on time. (Not only because the next activity is a

<15>

boisterous one, but also because if it is very long children will try to read the Bible for that length of time at home, fail, and give up). If an interesting question comes up and you run out of time, suggest that you continue talking about it next day. Above all, let the Holy Spirit be God rather than wanting to be God yourself! Don't try to force a child to speak or pray or make a decision – that is the Holy Spirit's job. When he is ready, he will act! And if it all goes *horribly* wrong, then the Holy Spirit is still in charge and no leader has anything to blame himself or herself for. Every day there should be a chance to report back on how the groups have gone after the children have left. At this point all the leaders can share the weight of the groups which have been difficult to run, and those who are thrilled with what has happened in their groups can give away some of their excitement! [†]

<16>

## GLADIHOUND

This popular and messy game show is repeated every day. It begins with the children sitting with their leaders in their groups around the perimeter of the hall. Everyone will be given 60 seconds in which to make a group list (eg, a list of flavours of crisps, a list of people Jesus met, a list of TV soap operas). The children in the groups call out suggestions to their own leaders who write them down on a piece of paper. When time is up, the children return to the centre of the room. One leader per team comes to the front and they sit in a straight line facing the children. Behind them is an overhead projector and screen, switched off, but ready to be switched on later to reveal each leader's forfeit!

The game-show host goes along the line of leaders asking them to read something from their list. The leader has three seconds to read one of the suggestions his or her group has made (to be fair, they are *not* allowed to invent a new one, it must be one that the children thought of during the 60 seconds). If the leader repeats one that has already been said, has run out of suggestions on the list, fails to speak in three seconds, or says one that the host has never heard of, he or she is out – until only one person remains. That leader's group is the winner.

A leader who is out must choose a number between one and six (quickly, or it drags). This number seals her or his fate. The overhead projector is turned on to reveal what has been chosen. On the screen are the six words given below with exclamation marks next to them. There are also six cut-out digits – 1, 2, 3, 4, 5 and 6 – one next to each forfeit (see below for cut-out templates). The forfeit is administered speedily, noisily and with no mercy! The overhead projector is then switched off and the digits rearranged so that the next leader who has to select one has no idea of what the consequences of their choice will be.

**Boooo!** A shameful boo until the leader has returned to his or her place.

**Aaaah!** A sympathetic sigh as the leader goes back to the group.

**Lucky!** The group survives until next round.

**Sweets!** The leader must give each member of his or her own group a (cheap!) sweet next time they meet.

**Crawl!** The leader must return to his or her place on hands and knees.

**Custard pie!** No need for explanation.

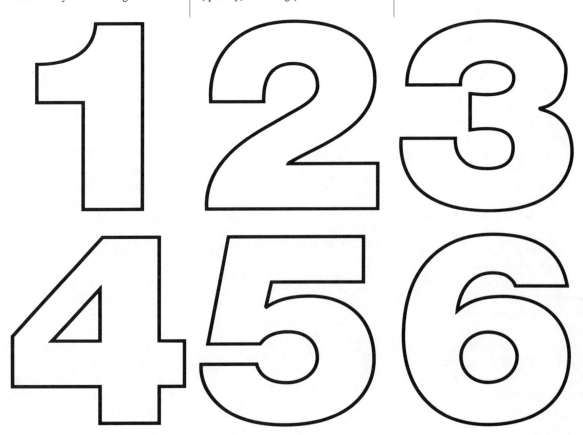

# HOUNDAROUND

This section of the programme allows the opportunity for one leader each day to give a testimony. These should be unspectacular stories of how they make Christianity work in practice. They should take place in a 'chat show' format, with the same person interviewing a different leader each day. Armchairs or stools should be used in the style of a television chat show, so this bears very little resemblance to the way testimonies are usually given in a church. The interviewer should ask a mixture of questions about all areas of the subject's interests, work, family, reasons for being part of the club, and questions about his or her Christian faith should be introduced in a matter of fact way, as of equal interest to the person's favourite colour or the names of his or her pets. Showing how following Jesus makes a practical difference to the day-to-day life of the adults whom the children are getting to know is a key element in the programme's impact, and it would be good to ensure that the people interviewed are *not* those who have a particularly visible role as an organiser of the club.

# THE REALLY KICKING HOUND SHOW

Although it should be introduced as if it were a *Top of the Pops*-type music broadcast, this is, in fact, a lively and joyful time of praise to God, interspersed with prayers. Since praise and prayer are quite serious matters, there is no need to overdo the similarity with a TV show at this point, although that need not mean it is not still exciting. The musicians should teach songs carefully, assuming that they will be unknown to the children, who may never have been to the church before. Include the *Newshounds* song, and repeat the same few songs again and again, so that they become familiar. Among the songs suggested each day, the action songs are particularly appropriate, but reflective songs should not

be excluded. When it comes to prayers, it should be explained to whom we are speaking and why. The suggested prayers grow in complexity and involvement as days go by. Written permission must be obtained from the publishers of songs whose words are written on charts or displayed on an overhead projector.

The words of many songs and hymns may be covered by the Church Copyright Licence for local church reproduction. The licence covers the words of over 100,000 worship songs and hymns for over 900 copyright owners. For a small annual fee, according to the size of the main congregation, the licence permits the church to reproduce these words onto overhead projector acetates, in service bulletins, songsheets, songbooks produced by the church for its own use and other word reproduction activities. Full details of the licence can be obtained from **Christian Copyright Licensing Ltd, PO Box 1339, Eastbourne, East Sussex BN21 4YF. Telephone (0323) 417711.**

# STUDIO DIALOGUES

As before, these scripted pieces of dialogue follow without introduction. They round the events of the day off, leaving the children anticipating the events of the next meeting of the club.

# CLOSEDOWN

If the club is being extended to include craft activities, this is the most suitable point to bring them into the programme. There are suggestions for newspaper-related crafts and hobbies on pages 18–23 of the book and, for some children, the opportunity to take part in developing the next day's newspaper with reporting, drawing, photography and other contributions could come at this point.

When the end of the session has been reached, the overall coordinator should close by briefly giving any notices, saying goodbye to the children. Since the leaders are responsible for the children's welfare, make sure that they leave with the correct adult and that no one leaves

unaccompanied or with someone whom they were not expecting would collect them (unless you are absolutely satisfied that this is their parents' intention). If adults have arrived early, invite them to watch the last few minutes of the programme standing at the back of the hall.

When all the children have gone, the leaders should interrupt the clearing up. They should sit down together and reflect on the day's programme. What worked well and what could be improved? Did the children discover what you hoped they would and what modifications to the programme are needed? Which children need specific prayers and for what can you give thanks to God? Follow this with a time of prayer. If the club is in the evening, look ahead to the teaching of the next day (or week) and study the Bible passage. Go on to talk about what practical preparations are required for the next session. Then finish clearing up and get the hall as ready as possible for the next session, freeing yourselves to spend the minutes before the children arrive in prayer rather than in panic!

# ALL-AGE SERVICE

A good climax to the event would be an all-age service to which whole families may come alongside the children who have attended the club. This service need not take place on the Sunday morning in church. It could happen on the final day of the club (eg on Friday evening) or on the day after (on the Saturday). Although the service may well take place in a different room, try to preserve some of the joyful atmosphere of the club. The service should prominently involve adults whom the children have come to know, songs which have been sung, and many references to the *Newshounds* newspapers. Invitations should be sent home with children towards the end of the week and, of course, an item about it could appear on the inside pages of the newspaper. An outline appears on page 62.

# News-craft activities

<18>

The club can be extended to include craft activities and it is particularly appropriate if they are selected to suit the newspaper theme, either by making contributions to *The Daily Hound*, or by making decorative or functional craft-work.

## Reporting

Children should be involved in as many stages and decisions as possible. They could write about something they have enjoyed during the day, devise a list of questions and then interview one of the leaders, review a part of the show, give comments and advice, tell a story, and so on. When they have developed their ideas thoroughly, allow them to do their own typing or word processing and make decisions about where their article should fit on the page. Give them constructive criticism on their work and help them think about what makes a good piece of writing that their friends would want to read. Encourage the habit of doing a second draft. Be honest with children about whether their finished work will definitely appear in the newspaper, so that they do not feel betrayed if their articles do not appear.

## Photography

A very small group is best for this, since careful supervision is needed. Discuss with the children who opt for this what makes a good photograph so that they are learning techniques rather than snapping randomly. If possible, use an SLR camera so that children can develop useful skills. Make selection part of the process by encouraging them to take multiple shots of their subject and discussing which one is best for the newspaper when they have been developed the next day.

## Drawing

Cartoon strips, graphics, logos, portraits, caricatures, statistical graphs, impressions of Bible stories and many other kinds of drawing are suitable for inclusion in the magazine; but be sure that children understand what will photocopy well in black and white and what detail will be lost. As with reporting and photography, involve children in deciding how their work can best be used in *The Daily Hound*.

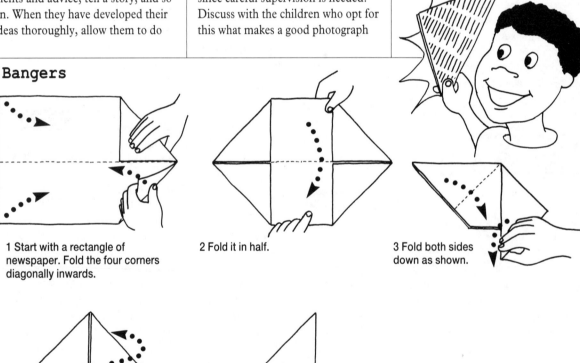

## Bangers

1 Start with a rectangle of newspaper. Fold the four corners diagonally inwards.

2 Fold it in half.

3 Fold both sides down as shown.

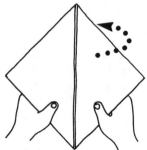

4 Fold it in half, backwards.

5 Hold the bottom points between your finger and thumb.

To make the banger work, hold it above your head and swing your arm downwards very hard. The inside pocket pops out making a loud enough bang to make most leaders wish they had never suggested it! To make it work again, push the inside pocket back in.

# Papier-mâché

Tear strips of newspaper and thoroughly soak them in wallpaper paste. This can then be used in many kinds of model making.

• Attach five paper cups to an inflated balloon so that they resemble the legs and snout of a pig. Cover it with the papier-mâché, several layers thick. Leave it to dry (this always takes longer than you think, more than overnight). Stick a pin in it to burst the balloon. Paint the pig pink, cut a slot in the top and create a piggy bank.

• Cover the inside of a pudding bowl with *Vaseline*. Overlap strips on top of the *Vaseline* until it is coated ten layers thick. Wait for it to dry, then turn it out and trim the edge. Paint and varnish it to make a sweet bowl.

• Cover half a balloon in the same way to make a mask, adding a nose-shaped blob of *Plasticine* for extra effect. Cut out eye holes and attach strings to tie at the back.

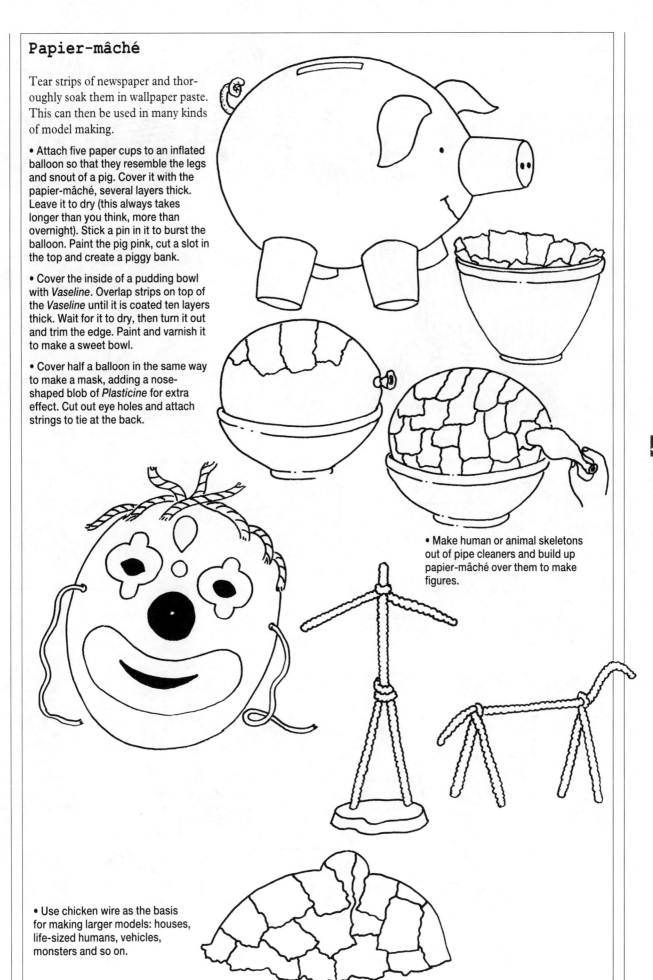

<19>

• Make human or animal skeletons out of pipe cleaners and build up papier-mâché over them to make figures.

• Use chicken wire as the basis for making larger models: houses, life-sized humans, vehicles, monsters and so on.

# Hats

Follow the instructions below to make one of several designs of newspaper hat.

<20>

## Crown

1 Start with a large square of paper, and fold it in half.

2 Fold it in half a second and then a third time.

3 Fold the two outer flaps inwards to meet in the middle.

4 Slide one hand between the edges of one flap. Open it out, pressing the top down, as shown.

5 Do the same to the other flap.

6 Turn everything over and fold the two outer flaps inwards, as shown.

7 Fold the two bottom corners of the top layer diagonally upwards to meet in the middle. Hold them in place with sticky tape.

8 Fold this bit so that the point meets the top edge in the middle.

9 Turn everything over and repeat steps 7 and 8 on the reverse side.

Finally pull the sides of your hat apart, pushing the middle section down so that the pointy bits stand out.

# Admiral's hat

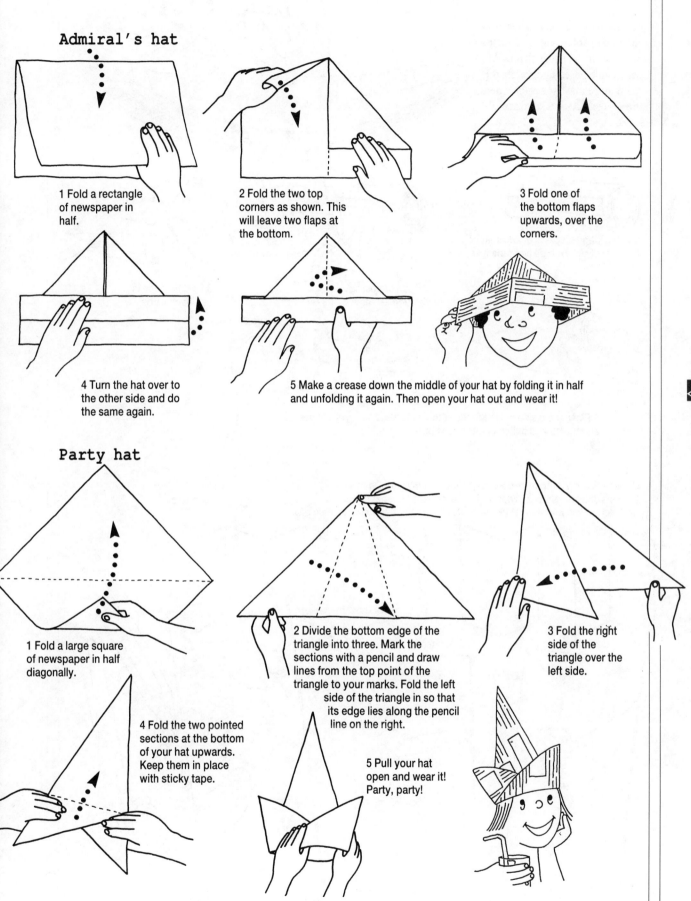

1 Fold a rectangle of newspaper in half.

2 Fold the two top corners as shown. This will leave two flaps at the bottom.

3 Fold one of the bottom flaps upwards, over the corners.

4 Turn the hat over to the other side and do the same again.

5 Make a crease down the middle of your hat by folding it in half and unfolding it again. Then open your hat out and wear it!

# Party hat

1 Fold a large square of newspaper in half diagonally.

2 Divide the bottom edge of the triangle into three. Mark the sections with a pencil and draw lines from the top point of the triangle to your marks. Fold the left side of the triangle in so that its edge lies along the pencil line on the right.

3 Fold the right side of the triangle over the left side.

4 Fold the two pointed sections at the bottom of your hat upwards. Keep them in place with sticky tape.

5 Pull your hat open and wear it! Party, party!

<21>

# Decorations

Create rows of animals, clowns and children by following the directions below, or make paper chains. All these can be used to decorate the room, or to make the room where the all-age service takes place spectacular.

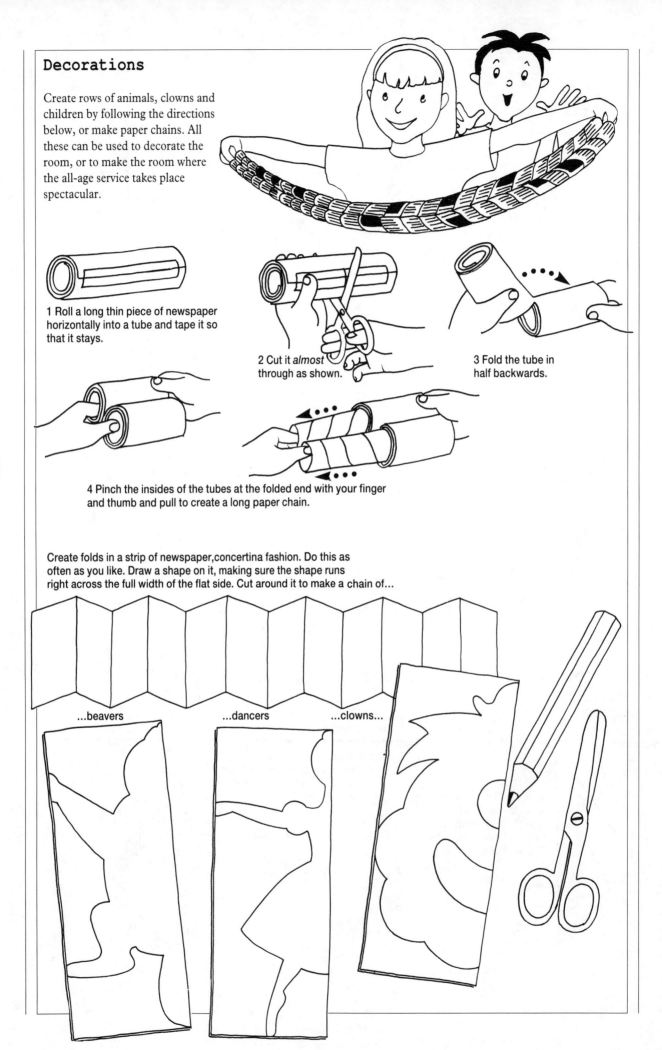

1 Roll a long thin piece of newspaper horizontally into a tube and tape it so that it stays.

2 Cut it *almost* through as shown.

3 Fold the tube in half backwards.

4 Pinch the insides of the tubes at the folded end with your finger and thumb and pull to create a long paper chain.

Create folds in a strip of newspaper, concertina fashion. Do this as often as you like. Draw a shape on it, making sure the shape runs right across the full width of the flat side. Cut around it to make a chain of...

...beavers        ...dancers        ...clowns...

<22>

# Slippers

A really useful craft if the club takes place during a rainy or snowy week!

1 Fold a rectangular sheet of newspaper in half vertically. Turn and fold the top of the strip inwards twice, as shown.

2 Turn it over and divide into three sections, as shown. Fold the right section in.

<23>

3 Hook a finger into the folded flap and pull it out a little, squashing it down to make it stick out slightly.

4 Fold the left section in. Pull the folded flap out a little, as before.

5 Holding the top part down (to keep it all together), bring the bottom edge to the top.

6 Tuck the bottom edge under the flap.

7 Keep everything together by sticking the flaps down with sticky tape.

Make another slipper. Turn them both over and they are ready to wear!

# After Newshounds

<24>

## RECORD KEEPING

Immediately after the event, details of children's names and addresses should be collated from the record cards so that a database can be set up. This means that children can be sent a personal invitation to any events that follow up the holiday club. The sending of a birthday card to every participating child is also a possibility.

## PERSONAL CONTACT

Most children enjoy receiving letters. Group leaders could be encouraged to write to those for whom they have been responsible, referring back to their shared experience of *Newshounds*. Such letters should be low key, and comments about the way a child developed spiritually during the week should not be made in a way that parents would find threatening or mysterious. Any invitation to meet the child again should be completely above suspicion.

## MIDWEEK CLUBS

An after-school or early-evening club may prove popular. It should contain a *Newshounds*-style mix of games, craft and Christian teaching. Scripture Union's Sound and Vision Unit produces a range of videos and accompanying activity material suitable for children without a great deal of Christian background, and there are many other resource publications listed below in 'Other Resources'. For a catalogue, write to the **Marketing Department, Scripture Union, 130 City Road, London EC1V 2NJ**. Mention that your church has been following the *Newshounds* programme, and specify whether you want a video or book catalogue.

## FAMILY EVENTS

By sending children to a holiday club, some parents who have no other connection with a church become a kind of 'fringe' to the congregation through this first involvement. A non-threatening recreational event for all ages together would bring them into contact with Christian people in a more relaxed way than a church service. This could be a barn dance, a barbecue, a sports day, a firework party, a karaoke evening, a treasure hunt, a swimming party, an outing, an arts and crafts afternoon, and so on. It should be an active time (not, for example, a video during which no one talks to anyone else) and the Christian content should be implicit rather than explicit (a well-constructed prayer of thanks before a meal, perhaps). The aim of these events is not to give an evangelistic challenge but to build relationships. In the context of friendships formed at events like these it becomes easier to invite someone to a service (maybe at Christmas) and, in the grace of God, people on the fringe of a church sometimes become part of its congregation – and create a new fringe among their own friends!

## SUNDAY CHILDREN'S MINISTRY

Children who have enjoyed a regular midweek club may grow in their understanding of the Christian faith to such an extent that a weekly Sunday morning programme is suitable for them. Scripture Union's SALT Programme offers a structured scheme of Bible teaching, application to life, praise and prayer. Whilst not as formal as a traditional 'Sunday School', its flexible, interactive package of stories, discussions, games and craft provides foundation teaching and worship for children of all ages, and a parallel programme for adults and 'family' services. Details of the scheme and sample materials can be obtained from the **SALT Programme coordinator, Scripture Union, 130 City Road, London EC1V 2NJ.** Specify whether your main interest is in:

- *SALT: 3 to 4+*, with *Sparklers* activity leaflets
- *SALT: 5 to 7+*, with *All Stars* activity leaflets
- *SALT: 8 to 10+*, with *Trailblazers* activity leaflets
- *SALT: 3 to 4+*, with *Lazer* activity magazine
- *SALT: all ages*, for all-age 'family' services and coordinated adult sermons

## OTHER RESOURCES

- *Splash!* – activities for under 5s.
- *Bounce!* – activities for 5-7s.
- *Springboard!* – activities for 7-11s.
- *Launchpad!* – activities for 11-14s.
- *You're Only Young Once! (YOYO!)* – four volumes of activities for teenage youth clubs.
- *Under Fives Welcome* – by Kathleen Crawford, about working with that age group in church.
- *Become like a Child* – by Kathryn Copsey, about working with 5-7s.
- *Help! There's a Child in my Church!* – by Peter Graystone, about working with 7-11s
- *A Church for All Ages* – by Peter Graystone and Eileen Turner, resource and information about all-age 'family' worship.
- *The Bumper Book of Family Activities* – by John Marshall, a good selection of ideas for all-age events.
- *Reaching Children* – by Paul Butler, about children's evangelism.
- *Outside In* – by Mike Breen, about reaching unchurched teenagers.
- *Let's Praise and Pray, Let's Join In, Praise God Together* – song books in which most of the listed songs can be found.

*Would You Like to Know Jesus?* – by Eira Reeves, explains the basics of Christian belief to under 8s.

## OTHER SCRIPTURE UNION HOLIDAY CLUB BOOKS

*The J Team* – by Peter Graystone (1990), is a basic introduction to the life of Jesus for use with those who have barely any Bible knowledge or Christian background.

*The Light Factory* – by Angela Flynn and Janet Morgan (1991), presents Jesus, the Light of the world, in a lively, sometimes zany, programme for children in churches.

*Shipshapes* – produced by the Scripture Union Missions Department (1992), follows the story of Peter through the Gospels and Acts. It is a traditional holiday club, with an accompanying video.

*Bodybuilders* – by Peter Graystone (1993), is a work-out, spiritual, physical and mental! It tells the whole story of the good news of God's dealings with his people for children who are not used to hearing Bible stories.

*On Fire!* – by Angela Flynn and Susan Currie (1994), introduces the Holy Spirit by looking at what happened to the disciples after Jesus' ascension. An off-beat event, it comes with an accompanying video and children's comics.

# The Newshounds logo

The logo may be used to raise the profile of the holiday club, on publicity material, T-shirts, press passes, badges and so on. Within the club, too, use it to give children a sense of belonging. Further publicity material, designed specially for this programme, is available from the **Christian Publicity Organisation, Garcia Estate, Canterbury Road, Worthing, West Sussex BN13 1BW.**

<25>

# The Newshounds song

## Put it on the front page
### (The Newshounds Theme)
Words and music: Derek Llewellyn

<26>

(Verse)
Of every story, that ever has been told,
In all the newspapers that ever have been sold,
The story of Jesus is the greatest in the world,
The news about Jesus for every boy and girl.

(Chorus)
So put it on the front page; Jesus makes you brand new,
Put it on the front page, Jesus loves me and you.

# The Daily Hound

**The Newshounds newspaper**     Issue **1**

# Stranger in wedding sensation!

Who exactly is this man Jesus? Why is he gathering a group of followers around him? In the first of a major new series our reporter John has set out to separate the truth from the rumours.

THERE WAS a wedding in the town of Cana in Galilee. Jesus' mother was there. Jesus and his followers were also invited to the wedding. When all the wine was gone, Jesus' mother said to him, 'They have no more wine.'

Jesus answered, 'Dear woman, why come to me? My time has not yet come.'

His mother said to the servants, 'Do whatever he tells you to do.'

## Reception embarrassment

In that place there were six stone water jars. The Jews used jars like these in their wedding ceremony. Each jar held about 100 litres.

Jesus said to the servants, 'Fill the jars with water.' So they filled the jars to the top.

Then he said to them, 'Now take some out and give it to the master of the feast.'

## Astonishing change

So the servants took the water to the master. When he tasted it, the water had become wine.

He did not know where the wine came from. But the servants who brought the water knew.

The master of the wedding called the bridegroom and said to him, 'People always serve the best wine first. Later, after the guests have been drinking a lot, they serve the cheaper wine.

But you have saved the best wine till now.'

## First reactions

So in Cana of Galilee, Jesus did his first miracle. There he showed his glory, and his followers believed in him.

Then Jesus went to the town of Capernaum with his mother, brothers and his followers. They all stayed in Capernaum for a few days.

Reporter: John
Source: International Children's Bible
References: Chapter 2, verses 1 to 12

# The Hound asks...

## For Hunky Hounds

1 In some places people with the skin disease leprosy are sent away from home. No one goes near them because they (mistakenly) think they can catch the disease by being near. What kinds of people can you think of today whom everyone avoids?

2 What does it tell you about Jesus that he spent time with someone that no one else would go near? How would Jesus react to the people on the list you have just made?

3 Why do you think only one of the ten people came back to thank Jesus? Ask your leader to tell you about one thing in his or her life for which he or she is really thankful to God. Then anyone else can say the things they are thankful for too.

## For Wee Hounds

1 What sort of things could the man do after he was healed that he could not do when he was sick?

2 What do you think Jesus felt about the man who came back to say thank you to him? What do you think he felt about the nine people who didn't bother to say thank you?

3 Ask your leader to tell you about one thing in his or her life for which he or she is really thankful to God.

## What's your reaction?
**For Hunky Hounds and Wee Hounds.**

Think of some of the things for which you want to say thank you to Jesus. Everyone who wants to can tell Jesus what they feel. Put the ideas you thought of into this sentence:

'Lord Jesus, thank you for

..............................................

..............................................

Amen.'

One at a time, say the sentence to him. Then your leader will say a prayer about the *Newshounds* club.

# PUZZLE PAGE

Go through the maze to see how the sick man changed when Jesus healed him.

**Hunky Hounds,** solve the codes to find out what Jesus and the man said.

1=A  2=B  3=C  4=D  5=E
6=F  7=G  8=H  9=I  10=J
11=K  12=L  13=M  14=N  15=O
16=P  17=Q  18=R  19=S  20=T
21=U  22=V  23=W  24=X  25=Y

**Wee Hounds,** follow the arrows to find out what the man said to Jesus.

Start here
16.18.1.9.19.5   7.15.4

_ _ _ _ _ _  _ _ _

Finish

25.15.21   1.18.5   8.5.1.12.5.4
2.5.3.1.21.19.5   25.15.21   2.5.12.9.5.22.5

_ _ _  _ _ _  _ _ _ _ _ _
_ _ _ _ _ _ _  _ _ _  _ _ _ _ _ _ _

# *The Daily Hound*

**The Newshounds newspaper**     Issue **3**

# Beggar's dream comes true

The excitement about Jesus is spreading further and further. Our reporter Mark is with the crowd following Jesus. He has been to Jericho where people ask, 'What will Jesus do next?'

THEY CAME to the town of Jericho. As Jesus was leaving there with his followers and a large crowd, a blind beggar named Bartimaeus (son of Timaeus) was sitting by the road.

## Blind since birth

He heard that Jesus from Nazareth was walking by. The blind man cried out, 'Jesus, Son of David, please help me!'

## Crowd angry

Many people scolded the blind man and told him to be quiet. But he shouted more and more, 'Son of David, please help me!'

Jesus stopped and said, 'Tell the man to come here.'

So they called the blind man. They said, 'Cheer up! Get to your feet. Jesus is calling you.' The blind man stood up quickly. He left his coat there and went to Jesus.

## Astonishing sight

Jesus asked him, 'What do you want me to do for you?'

The blind man answered, 'Teacher, I want to see again.'

Jesus said, 'Go! You are healed because you believed!'

At once the man was able to see again, and he followed Jesus on the road.

Reporter: Mark
Source: International Children's Bible
References: Chapter 10, verses 46 to 52

# The Hound asks...

## For Hunky Hounds

**1** Our reporter has failed to research what wrong things or sins the man had done. What kinds of wrong thing do you think it might have been?

**2** Why is it so important to have your sins forgiven? Would it matter if we just ignore the fact that Jesus can forgive us and carry on as we are?

**3** Ask whether, now your leader is a Christian, the change is so complete that he or she does not do things that need to be forgiven any more. What does he or she do about it when things go wrong? Then anyone who wants to can talk about times when they are glad they can say sorry to Jesus.

## For Wee Hounds

**1** What kinds of thing do we do wrong and need to say sorry for?

**2** Why do you think Jesus is so happy when we say sorry for the wrong things we have done?

**3** Ask whether, now your leader is a Christian, the change is so complete that he or she does not do things that need to be forgiven any more. What does he or she do about it when things go wrong?

## What's your reaction?
**For Hunky Hounds and Wee Hounds.**

Have a short silence during which everyone can think whether there is anything for which they need to say sorry to Jesus. Then the leader will count to three and everyone can say:

'Lord Jesus, I'm sorry. Please forgive me. Amen.'

Your leader will say a prayer thanking Jesus that he has forgiven and forgotten our sins. There may be other prayers that people want to say today as well.

---

**Hunky Hounds** can solve the puzzle on the right by writing down the words formed by the pictures. (It's easier if you go by the sound of the picture, not the spelling.) The message you have made comes from the Bible, the special book which contains the stories of Jesus. It comes from Acts chapter 10, verse 43.

**Wee Hounds** should colour in the shapes below that have a dot in them. It will show the name of the person who will forgive us for the wrong things we do every time we say sorry to him.

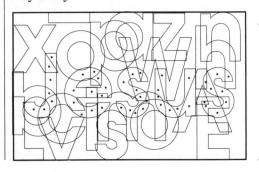

# PUZZLE PAGE

**Ever E 1**

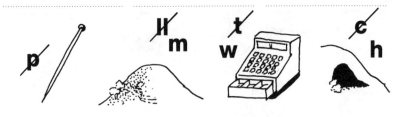

**4 given**

# Nasty little man's tax jackpot!

It is becoming clear that the country is divided in its attitude to Jesus. Some people claim that he has changed their lives for the better; others are turning their back on him or trying to get rid of him. Our reporter Luke met someone who has decided to stake everything on Jesus.

JESUS WAS going through the city of Jericho. In Jericho there was a man named Zacchaeus.

## Much hated figure

He was a wealthy, very important tax collector.

He wanted to see who Jesus was, but he was too short to see above the crowd. He ran ahead to a place where he knew Jesus would come.

## View from a tree

He climbed a sycamore tree so that he could see Jesus. When Jesus came to that place, he looked up and saw Zacchaeus in the tree. He said to him, 'Zacchaeus, hurry and come down! I must stay at your house today.'

Zacchaeus came down quickly. He was pleased to have Jesus in his house.

## Complaints give way to joy

All the people saw this and began to complain, 'Look at the kind of man Jesus stays with. Zacchaeus is a sinner.'

But Zacchaeus said to the Lord, 'I will give half of my money to the poor. If I have cheated anyone, I will pay that person back four times more!'

Jesus said, 'Salvation has come to this house today.'

Reporter: Luke
Source: International Children's Bible
References: Chapter 19, verses 1 to 9

Issue

# The Hound asks...

## For Hunky Hounds

1 Zacchaeus must have found it very difficult to give away his huge stacks of money. What do you think would be the hardest thing for you about following Jesus?

2 If you decide, like Zacchaeus, to be a follower of Jesus, where will the help you need come from?

3 Ask your leader what practical difference it makes to him or her to follow Jesus. What has been the best thing about it? Any regrets? Then anyone else in the group can talk about the best and worst things about following Jesus.

## For Wee Hounds

1 Do you think Zacchaeus enjoyed having Jesus as his friend? What sorts of thing do you think they did together?

2 If you are a friend of Jesus, what sorts of thing do you think he would want you to do?

3 Ask your leader what practical difference it makes to him or her to follow Jesus. What has been the best thing about it?

## What's your reaction?
### For Hunky Hounds and Wee Hounds.

Pray to Jesus about the things you have been chatting about. If it makes it easier, you can use this sentence:

'My friend Jesus, please help me to

......................................................

......................................................

Amen.'

One at a time, say the sentence to him. You can pray about anything else that is on your mind too. Then your leader will say a prayer for the whole group after the holiday club is over.

# PUZZLE PAGE

Zacchaeus has climbed a sycamore tree to get a better view of Jesus. But nobody seems to know where he has gone. Can you find him hidden in the tree?

**Hunky Hounds,** when you have tracked him down, see if you can find two squares in the picture that are absolutely identical.

**Wee Hounds,** decide which person in the picture you think is Jesus. Colour him in. Why did you choose that one?

# Roof destroyed in sin shocker!

Everyone who comes into contact with Jesus seems to be asking, 'Who is he?' Our reporter Luke has been at a gathering where Jesus answered the question in a powerful way. There was shock and anger from the Pharisees (religious leaders).

JESUS WAS teaching the people. The Pharisees and teachers of the law were there, too. They had come from every town in Galilee and from Judea and Jerusalem. The Lord was giving Jesus the power to heal people.

## Overcrowding fears

There was a man who was paralysed. Some men were carrying him on a mat. They tried to bring him in and put him down before Jesus. But because there were so many people there, they could not find a way to Jesus. So the men went up on the roof and made a hole in the ceiling. They lowered the mat so that the paralysed man was lying right before Jesus.

## Leaders shocked

Jesus saw that these men believed. So he said to the sick man, 'Friend, your sins are forgiven.'

The Jewish teachers of the law and the Pharisees thought to themselves, 'Who is this man? He is saying things that are against God! Only God can forgive sins.'

But Jesus knew what they were thinking. He said, 'Why do you have thoughts like that in your hearts? Which is easier: to tell this paralysed man, "Your sins are forgiven", or to tell him, "Stand up and walk"? But I will prove to you that the Son of Man has authority on earth to forgive sins.'

## Healing brings respect

So Jesus said to the paralysed man, 'I tell you, stand up! Take your mat and go home.'

Then the man stood up before the people there. He picked up his mat and went home, praising God. All the people were totally amazed and began to praise God. They were filled with much respect and said, 'Today we have seen amazing things.'

Reporter: Luke
Source: International Children's Bible
References: Chapter 5, verses 17 to 26

# The Hound asks...

## For Hunky Hounds

1 Why do you think the crowd tried to stop Bartimaeus from meeting Jesus?

2 What was it that made Bartimaeus follow Jesus down the road? What do you think he was expecting to happen if he followed Jesus?

3 Because Jesus is still alive in heaven today, he can still heal people who pray to him for help. Ask your leader if he or she can remember a time when Jesus answered a prayer. Then anyone else who wants to can tell the group about times when their prayers were answered.

## For Wee Hounds

1 What sorts of thing would you find it difficult to do if you could not see?

2 Why do you think Bartimaeus wanted to follow Jesus after he was made better?

3 Because Jesus is still alive in heaven today, he can still heal people who pray to him for help. Ask your leader if he or she can remember a time when Jesus answered a prayer.

## What's your reaction?
### For Hunky Hounds and Wee Hounds.

If Jesus asked *you* the question, 'What would you like me to do for you?', what would you reply? When you have thought about it for a moment, why not pray to him about it. Put the thing you thought of in this sentence:

'Please Jesus, ..................................

..................................

Amen.'

One at a time, say the sentence to him. Then your leader will say a prayer that Jesus will give us all those things that would be good for us.

# PUZZLE PAGE

Although our eyes are among the most precious things we have, sometimes they let us down – as you will see from these eye-boggling illusions.

## Narrow arrow

Which of these arrows is longer? A or B? Check by measuring!

## Dotty!

Which of the centre circles is bigger? C or D?

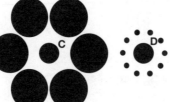

## Foot saw!

What does this say? Are you sure?

## Cricket wicket

Is this shape possible or impossible?

## Make the teacher disappear

Hold the page at arm's length and shut your left eye. Stare at the cross with your right eye and don't let your gaze wander off it. Slowly bring the page closer to your face. As you move it towards you, still focusing on the cross, the teacher will disappear from view, then reappear .

X

# The Daily Hound

**The Newshounds newspaper**

Issue **2**

# Amazing change for skin men!

Jesus is continuing his whirlwind tour of the area. Our reporter Luke caught up with him on the road to Samaria. This is a surprising place to find him, since Samaritan people have been hated for many years.

JESUS WAS on his way to Jerusalem. Travelling from Galilee to Samaria, he came into a small town.

## Jesus risks danger

Ten men met him there. These men did not come close to Jesus, because they all had a harmful skin disease. But they called to him, 'Jesus! Master! Please help us!'

## Dramatic healing

When Jesus saw the men, he said, 'Go and show yourselves to the priests.'

While the ten men were going, they were healed.

## Surprise gratitude

When one of them saw that he was healed, he went back to Jesus. He praised God with a loud voice. Then he bowed down at Jesus' feet and thanked him. (This man was a Samaritan.)

Jesus asked, 'Ten men were healed; where are the other nine? Is this Samaritan the only one who came back to thank God?' Then Jesus said to him, 'Stand up and go on your way. You were healed because you believed.'

Reporter: Luke
Source: International Children's Bible
References: Chapter 17, verses 11 to 19

# The Hound asks...

## For Hunky Hounds

**1** Reports seem to suggest that Jesus goes to a lot of parties like this. If he came to your party, what would you give him to eat and what kinds of activity do you think he would like to join in?

**2** What do you think Mary said to her friends when she saw what had happened?

**3** Ask your leader how he or she heard about Jesus for the first time, and who else has told him or her more as time has gone by. Then anyone else in the group who would like to can explain who first told them about Jesus.

## For Wee Hounds

**1** Jesus went to a lot of parties. If he came to your party, what would you give him to eat and what kinds of activity do you think he would like to join in?

**2** Why do you think people liked Jesus so much and wanted to be his friend?

**3** Ask your leader how he or she heard about Jesus for the first time, and who else has told him or her more as time has gone by.

## What's your reaction?
### For Hunky Hounds and Wee Hounds.

Think of some words which this story makes you feel about Jesus. Everyone who wants to can tell Jesus what they feel. Put the word you thought of in this sentence:

'Lord Jesus, you are

.........................................

.........................................

Amen.'

One at a time, say the sentence to him. Then your leader will say a prayer that you will have a really happy and safe day today.

# PUZZLE PAGE

Here is a picture of the twelve men who were the first to follow Jesus. They went with him to the wedding. Two of them were brothers and the sons of Zebedee. In the picture they have such a strong family likeness that they could be twins. Can you work out which two are the brothers?

**Wee Hounds** can colour in the two who are brothers.

**Hunky Hounds** can work out their names by matching the shapes below with the letters.

_ _ _ _ _

_ _ _ _

# Newshounds

## DAY–BY–DAY PROGRAMME OUTLINES

<39>

## Newshounds DAY 1

**STUDIO REPORT** Luke 4:14-44

The riot at Nazareth leads Jesus to set up home in Capernaum, where he becomes a popular religious leader.

**NEWSPAPER REPORT** John 2:1-12

Jesus performs a miracle at a wedding in Cana.

### 9.30 <6.15>
### Leaders' preparation

Pray that every leader will learn from God and be able to pass on what they know of God during this event as they take their place on the team. Then read Luke 4:4-44 and John 2:1-12, and discuss some or all of these questions:

**1** In the passage about the wedding at Cana, what do you think Mary was expecting when she spoke to Jesus in verse 3? What did she learn about Jesus from this incident? What are you hoping that children who come to the club will learn this week?

**2** In Luke 4:14-44, what different reactions did various people have to Jesus? What different reactions to Jesus are you expecting from the children at *Newshounds*?

**3** What do these verses tell us about why Jesus preached the good news about the Kingdom of God? Why is it that you have given up your time to share this good news with children?

Invite everyone in the group to share one thing they are looking forward to and one thing they are anxious about with regard to the *Newshounds* holiday club. Pray together about what you have heard.

NB. If the club takes place in the evening, use only the final prayers at this point, the Bible study having taken place on a previous occasion, as explained on page 13. Continue to adapt the preparation in this way, day by day.

### 10.15 <6.30>
### Opening credits

Welcome and register children, then lead them to their small groups in the way described on page 13. As children arrive at their group, give each one a **press pass**. The outline below may be photocopied straight from the page or used as the basis for a home-made card. This is for children to wear, either with a safety pin or round

<40>

## PRESS PASS
### IDENTITY

*Event*
**Newshounds**

*Day*
**One**

Name

These are the people and pets
who live at home

the neck with a ribbon, in order to identify them. The child's name should be written on the pass and felt-tipped pens provided so that it can be coloured, decorated and pictures of the people and pets who live at home with them drawn. Group leaders should use this time to talk to and take a more detailed record of each boy and girl.

## 10.30 <6.45>
## Headlines

As children gather to sit in the central seating area, a loud, excitement-raising jingle begins. This comes either from the *Newshounds–Location Report* video (before each episode), or from live musicians or a commercially produced compilation album of jingles and sound effects which can be purchased from a large record shop or borrowed from a library. At the end of it the link man takes his place and the presentation begins:

**Link man:** The time is (*correct time*). The date is (*today's date*). The place is the *Newshounds* holiday club. This is the news!

BBC television today announced the launch of a new soap opera. It is to feature a cast made up entirely of horses and sheep. The show is going to be called *Neighbaaas*.

A government report on school dinners shows that, in a recent survey, 99 per cent of children thought they tasted like glue.

Teachers are reported as saying they are sorry, but children are going to have to stick to them.

Scientists have announced that for the first time they have succeeded in crossing a fruit, an elephant, and a goldfish. As a result they have produced a pear of swimming trunks.

(Other news-jokes can be added which are specific to the club that is taking place, and leaders and children who are present.)

And now for news of today's *Newshounds* show, here's (*name of the overall coordinator*).

The co-ordinator should give a welcome to the children, raise their anticipation, and explain any details of the day's programme which need to be announced publicly. It is best to do this without breaking the illusion of a television production, so he or she could do this in the style of a continuity announcer.

## 10.35 6.50
## Studio dialogue

**Link man:** I am (*name*). That was the news. And now a word from our sponsors.
**Producer:** Hi (*name*)!
**Link man:** Quiet! I'm on air. The commercials are going out.
**Producer:** Since when has that bothered you? You're the man who forgot he had his radio mike on when he went to the toilet and broadcast the flush to the entire nation.
**Link man:** I didn't do it on purpose.
**Producer:** That's not what the coastguards said when they thought a tidal wave had hit Essex and closed the Thames flood barrier.

**Link man:** At least it got the nation laughing. I've broadcast so much bad news in the bulletins this year that you wonder whether there is anyone happy left in the world.
**Producer:** Feeling depressed?
**Link man:** Well, have you had any good news lately?
**Producer:** We've won a medal in the Rome Olympics!
**Link man:** Bronze. Everyone thought it was a failure.
**Producer:** The weather forecast is for the sunniest summer ever.
**Link man:** Yeah, but with the hole in the ozone layer, that's not such good news as it used to be.
**Producer:** There's a new newspaper on the market selling millions of copies!
**Link man:** I'm not surprised. It's called the *Bad Times*. That's all everybody wants to hear about.
**Producer:** There must be some good news out there.
**Link man:** Well, if there is, make sure you get out there and find it, because I'm fed up with introducing reporters who make the news depressing. You're the best television producer we've got. The news broadcast you produce, the Jake Newshound show, is the most popular in the country. If you can't find good news, no one can.
**Producer:** Look, there's a story breaking in Galilee. I'm not sure of the details yet, but it seems like there is a new religious leader who is giving people a new outlook on life. Should I check it out?
**Link man:** If it's a story worth telling, I'll have it on air tonight.
**Producer:** I'm away! Oh (*name*), can you have our religious affairs commentator on stand-by? If it's a big story, we'll want her to explain the significance.

<41>

**Link man:** (*As the producer exits.*) Will do. Later then! Got to go, they're counting me down into the sports programme....

## 10.40 <6.55>
## Aerobihound

The link man ad libs to the beginning of these simple and fast-moving exercises to music, as if he were a continuity announcer introducing a television programme: 'And now, the woman who put the skip into Skipton, the haste into Hastings, the run into Runcorn and the loo into Luton; that legendary, lively, leaping lady, (*name*).' Obviously, if the work-out leader is a man, the alliterations are mighty, muscle-bound, magnificent, and so on.

<42>

## 10.45 <7.00>
## *Newshounds–Location Report* video or *Good News at Ten* drama

If the video is being used, show episode one. If the broadcasts are being performed live, play the introductory music that announces Jake Newshound, Anne O'Pinion, and the pre-recorded 'eye-witness' interview:

'*Good News at Ten*. This is Jake Newshound reporting on the remarkable case of a new religious leader named Jesus. Our reporters have been following him ever since they heard of disturbances at the town of Nazareth.

'The man seems to have spent his childhood in this town, and has gained a growing reputation as a preacher in local synagogues. Apparently everyone who hears him speak about God is full of praise for the wise words he says and the lively way in which he communicates. Today, though, events seem to have taken a surprising turn, with angry scenes and violence narrowly avoided. Our outside broadcast unit in Nazareth sent this report on today's events.'

**Interviewer's voice:** I am speaking from outside the synagogue, and I have a lady here who witnessed all that happened today. Do you know Jesus well?

**Woman's voice:** Know him? My dear, I grew up with him. Everyone knows him – Mary and Joseph's son.

**Interviewer's voice:** And you respect him as a teacher?

**Woman's voice:** Indeed! And I

thought today would be like any other day. He was reading part of the Bible, all about good news for people – the poor, the sick, those who are miserable. He told us that God was at hand to save his people.

**Interviewer's voice:** What was the reaction?

**Woman's voice:** Wonderful at that stage! Everyone thought it was terrific.

**Interviewer's voice:** So what went wrong?

**Woman's voice:** Well, my dear, we are all so proud of being Jewish. We love God and we try to serve him. Not everyone does, my dear! We know God will save us one day – we're very special to him – and he'll rescue us from all the things that make our life difficult. It was fine while Jesus was saying that. But he started saying that God wasn't only going to rescue us Jewish people. That all this good news God is bringing isn't just for us, it's for *all* people in the world – people from Sidon, people from Syria … I mean, *where* will it all end?

**Interviewer's voice:** So the people in the congregation didn't like what Jesus was saying?

**Woman's voice:** Like it! They hated it! They dragged him off his seat and out into the town.

**Interviewer's voice:** Violently?

**Woman's voice:** My dear, I thought they were going to kill him. I thought they were going to throw him right over the cliff.

**Interviewer's voice:** But he escaped?

**Woman's voice:** Don't ask me how! Wriggled away! Clean through the middle of them!

**Interviewer's voice:** Do you know where he's gone to?

**Woman's voice:** Well, they say he's gone to Capernaum. Good luck to him!

**Interviewer's voice:** So you don't think we've heard the last of him then?

**Woman's voice:** I hope not! Believe me, there's something different about that man. Something only God can be responsible for. Wait and see, my dear! Wait and see!

**Interviewer's voice:** From an excited Nazareth back to the studio.

'Later reports confirmed that Jesus had gone to Capernaum, where remarkable events took place. As evening drew on, people who had friends that were sick began to bring them to Jesus to ask him to heal them. He placed his hands on them and prayed for them, and one by one each one was healed no matter what the disease was.

'Among the healed people was Simon's mother-in-law, who is reported to have had a high fever. It took only a visit from Jesus to her bedside to restore her to health, and Jesus has subsequently had a meal at her house. Much to everyone's surprise, he left the town before dawn this morning, moving on to neighbouring villages. When they realised he had slipped away, the people of Capernaum rushed after him to persuade him to stay, but he insists that God has sent him to do an important task, and that he must fulfil it. The task is to take the good news about God to the whole area.

'At this point let me introduce Anne O'Pinion, our religious affairs commentator. Anne, help us to understand these unusual events that are taking place. Have you found out anything about the background of this man Jesus?'

*(Anne O'Pinion's reply should briefly mention the circumstances of Jesus' birth and explain that he has grown up to be a wise and well-respected man.)*

'How do you think he is able to heal people in such a miraculous way?'

*(Anne's reply should talk about the power to heal people coming from God alone.)*

'Jesus does seem to be a good man. What else can you tell us about him as a person?'

*(Anne's reply should describe to the children what Jesus was like: his kindness to people, his care for individuals, the fact that he was good in every way.)*

'We keep hearing this phrase 'the good news about God'. What exactly is this good news?'

*(The reply should explain that God has a great love for all people whom he created, and a longing that they should be his friends. The good news is that there is nothing to stop adults and children following him: Jesus will show them the way.)*

'Thank you, Anne. I am quite sure we will be hearing more of Jesus as days go by. But for now, from Jake Newshound in Studio 2, back to the *Newshounds* Show.'

## 10.55 <7.10>
## The Daily Hound

The children go to their groups to receive, enjoy and talk about today's newspaper. Full instructions for preparing and running these group-times appear in the introductory section of this book, on pages 9-10 and 15).

## 11.15 <7.30>
## Gladihound

An explanation and the first round of the game show. Full instructions are given on page 16. The subject for today's list is...breakfast cereals.

## 11.30 <7.45>
## Houndaround

A 'chat show' style interview about the life, interests and Christian experience of one of the leaders. Advice for this section appears on page 17.

## 11.40 <7.55>
## The Really Kicking Hound Show

Songs that reflect today's theme without introducing confusing new concepts are listed below. (These songs can be found in the *Junior Praise* and *Praise God Together* songbooks.) Other songs may also be suitable if the children attending the club are used to coming to church and familiar with the ideas that the songs contain.

- The *Newshounds* song
- Jesus' love is very wonderful
- Jesus is a friend of mine
- We love to praise You, Jesus
- Jesus' hands were kind hands

At some point during the singing, use this chant as a prayer, the leader saying the alternate lines rhythmically and everyone replying with the repeated italic phrase:

When I see the Concorde flying,
*Life is lovely thanks to God,*
Sunset as the day is dying,

<43>

*Life is lovely thanks to God,*
Hear the roar of crowds at
Wembley,
*Life is lovely thanks to God,*
Roller-coasters turn me trembly,
*Life is lovely thanks to God,*
Trumpets sounding brash and
tinny,
*Life is lovely thanks to God,*
Hot baths round me bare and
skinny,
*Life is lovely thanks to God,*
Dewdrops hung on cobweb
wisps,
*Life is lovely thanks to God,*
Taste of ready salted crisps,
*Life is lovely thanks to God,*
Smell of eggs and bacon
cooking,
*Life is lovely thanks to God,*
Scratch an itch when no one's
looking,
*Life is lovely thanks to God,*
Staying up till late at night,
*Life is lovely thanks to God,*
Then I shout with all my might,
*Life is lovely thanks to God.*

This act of praise could also be
used:

**Leader**: Give me a J.
**Children**: J!
**Leader**: Give me a E.
**Children**: E!
**Leader**: Give me a S.
**Children**: S!
**Leader**: Give me a U.
**Children**: U!

**Leader**: Give me a S.
**Children**: S!
**Leader**: What do we get?
**Children**: Jesus.
**Leader**: What do we think of
him?
**Children**: (*Cheers and
clapping!*)

## 11.55 <8.10>
### Studio dialogue

**Link man:** And that was (*name*)
presenting today's *Really
Kicking Hound Show*. He'll be
back tomorrow with more of
your favourites. And now sit
back for tonight's big movie,
*Jurassic Hound*.
   Phew! That's it! I'm off air now
for two hours.
**Producer:** Time for a late night
bevvie?
**Link man:** OK! I expect that's
what most of the audience are
away to do.
**Producer:** I'm whacked! I've
seen some amazing sights
today, I can tell you!
**Link man:** The Jesus man!
What did you make of him?
Honestly? Now Jake
Newshound has finished his
broadcast and you're off air, you
can tell me.
**Producer:** Make of him? It's
too early to say. All I know is
that I shall be back there
tomorrow to find out what
happens.
**Link man:** Well, at least you
delivered good news, just like
you promised, no matter what
you make of him.
**Producer:** I wish you wouldn't
say that!
**Link man:** Why?
**Producer:** It's not what I make
of him that I'm worried about.
It's what he's going to make of
me.

## 12.00 <8.15>
### Closedown

The overall coordinator brings
the meeting to a close and says
goodbye to the children.

<44>

# Newshounds DAY 2

**STUDIO REPORT** Luke 6:46–7:50

Controversial sayings and actions win Jesus a huge following, but there is a rising tide of opposition.

**NEWSPAPER REPORT** Luke 17:11–19

As a man healed of a dreadful skin disease discovered, there is so much to thank Jesus for.

## 9.30 <6.15>
### Leaders' preparation

Pray that you will all learn today what it means to be obedient to Jesus, both from what you discuss now and from what the day's experience teaches you in practice. Then read Luke 6:46 – 7:10 and 17:11-19, and discuss some or all of these questions:

**1** Why was the thankfulness of the man in Luke 17:11-19 so important to Jesus? What have you got to be thankful for about the first session of *Newshounds*?

**2** What can the same passage teach us about the way we treat children whom we like instantly and those we find it hard to like? How can we make sure that we approach them with the same attitude that Jesus had?

**3** Read Luke 6:46-49 again. When *Newshounds* is over, how will you know whether it has been more like a house built on sand or a house built on rock?

Give thanks to God for the things you mentioned when you discussed question 1 and then go on to pray for today's activities.

## 10.15 <6.30>
### Opening credits

Welcome and register children, then lead them to their groups. On today's press pass, children should draw and colour things that they enjoy doing – their favourite activities, toys, games and entertainments.

## 10.30 <6.45>
### Headlines

The children gather, the jingle plays at an exciting volume and the presentation begins:

**Link man:** The time is (*correct time*). The date is (*today's date*). The place is the *Newshounds* holiday club. This is the news!

There was uproar at St Stupid's Hospital today when a doctor

<45>

---

# PRESS PASS
### IDENTITY

*Event*
**Newshounds**

*Day*
**Two**

*Name*
...................................

These are the things
I most enjoy doing

announced that he had good news and bad news for a man who had been admitted to have his leg cut off. The bad news was that the surgeons accidentally cut off the wrong leg. The good news was that the other one had got better anyway.

Scientists reported today that they have developed the world's first ten-metre tall, yellow flower. It is called a girrafodil.

There was a catastrophe in the North Sea this morning when a ship carrying blue paint collided with a ship carrying red paint. The entire cargo of both ships has been emptied into the sea. The crew have been marooned.

*(Other localised news-jokes can be added.)*

And now for news of today's *Newshounds* Show, here is (*name of the overall co-ordinator*).

The co-ordinator welcomes the children and announces any notices that need to be given.

## 10.35 <6.50>
## Studio dialogue

**Link man:** I am (*name*). That was the news. And now, for children, *The Magic Houndabout*. (*Producer enters.*) Oh hi, guy! You're looking cool!
**Producer:** Anything but cool tonight, (*name*). Red hot tonight!

**Link man:** Well, you're certainly making an impact around here. Do you know how many people tuned into Jake Newshound's broadcast last night?
**Producer:** How many?
**Link man:** 5000.
**Producer:** Good grief. I'll tell you something even more amazing. That's about how many people turned up this lunchtime to hear Jesus' Lake Galilee sermon.
**Link man:** The crowds are obviously hungry to hear him.
**Producer:** Not only hungry to hear him, hungry to eat as well. And stone me, the catering team managed to feed them all using just five loaves and two fish.
**Link man:** Are you joking?
**Producer:** No, not joking. Describing a miracle.

**Link man:** So what are you reporting on tonight?
**Producer:** I'm back to Capernaum. There's something strange about that man. I mean, it's not just that he has such authority when he speaks, it's... I don't know... It's something more than human.
**Link man:** Make it a good one, (*name*).
**Producer:** Ciao! (*He goes.*)
**Link man:** That was *The Little Hound on the Prairie*. And for those of you still awake, time for a little keep fit.

## 10.40 <6.55>
## Aerobihound

The link man could ad lib in this manner: 'And now, the lady with the hop of a grasshopper, the spring of a springbok, the hips of a hippopotamus and the bum of a bumble bee, the practically priceless, princess presenter of Aerobihound, (*name*).'

## 10.45 <7.00>
## *Newshounds—Location Report* video or *Good News at Ten* drama

If the video is being used, show episode two. If the broadcasts are being performed live, play the introductory music that announces Jake Newshound, Anne O'Pinion, and the pre-recorded 'eye-witness' interview:

'*Good News at Ten*. This is Jake Newshound reporting on the Jesus phenomenon.

'The centre of attention today has been the towns near Lake Galilee, where Jesus has been preaching. He has now gathered around him a special team of helpers, twelve of them. The all-male team travel with him everywhere.

'Near Capernaum a large crowd gathered to hear one of the stories which have become so much a part of Jesus' style. He told of a builder who dug deep foundations into hard earth and has created a house that was safe in all weathers and circumstances. In contrast, another builder cut corners and skimped expensive detail by building without foundations on sandy soil. Apparently, in storms this house was completely destroyed, although the house

<46>

with stone foundations is still waterproof and providing good shelter for the family. Jesus would not be drawn into explaining the meaning of the story, although he explained that disobeying him was the equivalent of building without foundations on sand.

'Striding manfully along the road, he arrived in Capernaum where a remarkable healing took place. This eye-witness account comes direct from the scene.'

**Interviewer's voice:** Sir, thank you for sparing time to talk to us. I understand that you are an army man?

**Man's voice:** An officer indeed. I'm used to giving orders. No nonsense from anyone.

**Interviewer's voice:** And you are a good friend to the Jewish community here?

**Man's voice:** Indeed. I built their synagogue for them. I like these people. I sense they respect me.

**Interviewer's voice:** But you have a great sadness in your life!

**Man's voice:** Not any more I haven't. Not any more!

**Interviewer's voice:** What has happened?

**Man's voice:** This time yesterday I had a servant who was so ill that I thought he was going to die. He is a very dear friend. I was beside myself with worry for him. I head that Jesus was in town so I sent a message asking him to heal the man.

**Interviewer's voice:** And he came to your house?

**Man's voice:** No, no! I couldn't possibly have someone like Jesus in my house. He is far too great to visit someone like me.

**Interviewer's voice:** But surely you are a man with great authority?

**Man's voice:** You don't know what you are saying. Next to

Jesus, we are all nothing. Nothing! I sent friends to tell him not to stoop to come to me, but just to give the order. I knew my servant would be made well.

**Interviewer's voice:** And is he well?

**Man's voice:** Never been better. Leapt out of bed like a new man. He's polishing my armour this very minute.

**Interviewer's voice:** Have you thanked Jesus?

**Man's voice:** I never got to meet him. You don't have to see someone like that in person. You just know. And you worship. And you obey. I recognise authority when I see it.

**Interviewer's voice:** A wonderful story! Thank you for taking time to be with us, sir.

**Man's voice:** Pleasure!

**Interviewer's voice:** Now back to the studio.

'At a party hosted by Simon, one of the most respected religious leaders in Capernaum, a controversial incident took place.

'In a moment of great drama the meal was interrupted by a woman who rushed in and flung herself at Jesus' feet, sobbing with emotion. She poured expensive perfume on Jesus' bare feet and, as the tears cascaded onto his toes, she wiped them away with her hair.

'Party guests stood back in embarrassment, since she is known locally as a notorious wrong-doer. They looked to see whether Jesus would treat this much-hated woman in the style she deserved. However, they were astonished when he rounded on them and reprimanded their bad attitude: "This woman has shown that her love for me is far greater than yours!"

'There were gasps as he said to the woman, "I forgive all your sins." People were clearly outraged because forgiving sins is something that only God can do. Jesus said to the woman, "You are saved because you believe in me. Go in peace."

'Anne O'Pinion, religious affairs correspondent for *Good News at Ten*, I think a word from you now would help us understand this better. Jesus' story about builders, encouraging people to make firm foundations – what do you make of that?'

*(Anne O'Pinion's reply should explain that it isn't really about houses at all. It is about making sure that whatever happens in your life, Jesus is a part of it by obeying him, rather than risking any other way.)*

'People are saying that Jesus has authority when he speaks. What kind of authority do you think that is?'

*(Anne's reply should say that she has come to the conclusion that Jesus is God himself, living on earth. Only God could do such things.)*

'This remarkable business about Jesus forgiving sins – surely he can't forgive the ordinary wrong things that people do, can he?'

*(Anne's reply should explain how we can say sorry to Jesus for the wrong things we do day by day, and that he will always forgive us and welcome us back as his friends.)*

'Thank you, Anne, for those wise and encouraging words. And now goodnight from Anne and me, Jake Newshound, in Studio 2.'

## 10.55 <7.10>
### The Daily Hound

The children go to their groups for today's newspaper.

## 11.15 <7.30>
### Gladihound

Today's round of the game show. The subject for the list is…flavours of crisps.

## 11.30 <7.45>
### Houndaround

Another interview with one of the leaders.

## 11.40 <7.55>
### The Really Kicking Hound Show

Songs which were taught yesterday should be repeated so that children who do not know any Christian songs become familiar with a few rather than be confused by many. If a new song is taught today, it should reflect today's theme. Suitable songs include:

- The *Newshounds* song
- The wise man built his house upon the rock
- Don't build your house on the sandy land
- Thank You, thank You, Jesus
- Thank you, Lord, for this fine day
- Get up out of bed
- O give thanks to the Lord, all you His people

(These songs can be found in the *Junior Praise*, *Praise God Together* and *Let's Join In!* songbooks.) At some point during the singing say this prayer, the leader saying each line and the children repeating it:

Thank you, God, for Jesus…
Thank you for the wise things he said…
Thank you for the kind things he did…
Thank you for the loving way he made friends…
Thank you for the amazing way he healed people…
Thank you, God, for Jesus…
Lord Jesus, you are the best…

Ask everyone to think how they would finish the sentence, 'Lord Jesus, you are…'. After a moment to decide on an appropriate ending, invite them to tell the person next to them what they have decided. Then introduce a shout of praise, with everyone declaring together, 'Lord Jesus, you are…' and completing the sentence in their own way.

## 11.55 <8.10>
### Studio dialogue

**Link man:** (*As producer enters.*) Hi (*name*). Give me ten, I've got to introduce the movie. Three, two, one… And now for all of you who are children at heart, tonight's big film, *Beauty and the Hound*.
**Producer:** I just came to say goodnight.
**Link man:** Lucky man. I'm on air until midnight.
**Producer:** Leave it out. I haven't exactly been dabbling my toes in the Jordan all day. I've been tracking Jesus since dawn.
**Link man:** He's a rising star, isn't he? They say nothing could stop him if he gathered an army round him.
**Producer:** That's not his style, at least I don't think it is.
**Link man:** Does he look to you like a man who could be king?
**Producer:** No one can stop him. At least, he might stop himself.
**Link man:** How do you mean?
**Producer:** He's saying some dangerous things. He'll be making enemies, I'm sure.
**Link man:** Enemies?
**Producer:** Oh, maybe not. Let's talk about it tomorrow. Goodnight.
**Link man:** Goodnight.

## 12.00 <8.15>
### Closedown

The overall coordinator brings the meeting to a close and says goodbye to the children.

<48>

# Newshounds DAY 3

**STUDIO REPORT** Luke 19:28-48
(Matthew 21:15-16)
Jesus enters Jerusalem, making a specific claim of kingship, exposing hypocrisy in the Pharisees and charlatanism in Temple trade, much to the anger of the priests.

**NEWSPAPER REPORT** Mark 10:46-52
As a blind beggar found out, we can pray to Jesus asking for the things we need.

## 9.30 <6.15>
### Leaders' preparation

Praise Jesus as King of the holiday club and all its participants. Then read Luke 19:28-48 and Mark 10:46-52, and discuss some or all of these questions:

**1** If Jesus asked you, as he did in Mark 10:51, 'What do you want me to do for you?', what would you reply? And what do you most want him to do for the children?

**2** Matthew 21:15-16 tells us that what really upset the priests about Jesus' entry into Jerusalem was that children were shouting exuberant praise of Jesus. Do you think children at *Newshounds* this week have got anything to teach the leaders about prayer?

**3** If it had been your city or town or village that Jesus had entered today, what would have made him weep (Luke 19:41)?

Invite any of the leaders to mention particular children in their groups who have come to their attention because of particular needs that they seem to have. Pray especially for them, and for other things that discussing question 1 has brought to mind.

## 10.15 <6.30>
### Opening credits

Welcome children, register them and take them to their groups. On today's press pass, children should draw and colour their favourite foods and drinks.

## 10.30 <6.45>
### Headlines

The children gather, the jingle plays at an exciting volume and the presentation begins:

**Link man:** The time is (*correct time*). The date is (*today's date*). The place is the *Newshounds* holiday club. This is the news!

Hospital news! A postman limped into the casualty department in

<49>

---

# PRESS PASS
### IDENTITY

*Event*
**Newshounds**

*Day*
**Three**

*Name*
...........................................

These are my favourite foods and drinks

the early hours of this morning. He said to the doctor, 'A dog's just bitten my leg.' 'Oh dear,' said the doctor. 'Did you put anything on it?' The postman replied, 'No, he liked it just as it was' ... The postman later got the sack.

At the *Newshounds* holiday club today it was reported that all the leaders were going to have to start wearing dark glasses. It is because all the children are so bright!

Scientists released news today of a dramatic experiment in which they have succeeded in crossing a monkey with a flower. They are calling the new creature a chimppansy.

*(Other localised news-jokes can be added.)*

And now for news of today's *Newshounds* show, here's (*name of the overall coordinator*).

The coordinator welcomes the children and announces any notices that need to be given.

## 10.35 <6.50>
## Studio dialogue

**Link man:** I am (*name*). That was the news. And now the Australian soap, *Hound and Away*.
**Producer:** (*Enters.*) What's the blag, (*name*)?
**Link man:** I don't know if it's good news or not. Your man's on his way to Jerusalem.
**Producer:** I know. I had a fax from the office in Jericho to get down there straight away.
**Link man:** What do you think he's after, this Jesus? Do you think he's about to make a move to overthrow the Roman army?
**Producer:** Can't tell. You ask a blind man who can see again, or a beggar who has heard the first

kind words spoken to him since he was a baby, and they'll say yes.
**Link man:** And you? What do you say?
**Producer:** I say that if I don't get to the gates of Jerusalem, the Producer from the *Bad Times* will scoop a story off me. See you later.
**Link man:** Go safely. Something tells me this is going to get dirty.
**Producer:** Gone already. (*Exit.*)

## 10.40 <6.55>
## Aerobihound

The link man ad libs: 'And now, she taught the Poles how to pole vault, she taught the Swiss how to swim, she taught the Russians how to rush, she taught the Gulf to play golf. She finished in Finland, she tied in Thailand, she went mad in Madagascar, and she never visited Nicaragua. Here she is, (*name*)!'

## 10.45 <7.00>
## *Newshounds–Location Report* video or *Good News at Ten* drama

If the video is being used, show episode three. If the broadcasts are being performed live, play the introductory music that announces Jake Newshound, Anne O'Pinion, and the pre-recorded 'eye-witness' interview:

'*Good News at Ten*. This is Jake Newshound reporting on the Jesus phenomenon.

'Attention switched this afternoon to Jerusalem where Jesus brought the entire town to a standstill. The town was crowded, since it is the day of the fruit market, and the dates and figs which come up from Jericho wrapped in palm leaves were on sale in the bazaar.

'At about three o'clock market-

stall holders became aware of jubilant noises outside the city gate getting louder and louder. Jerusalem residents are now used to the disruption caused by Jesus wherever he goes, but strangers watched the spectacle in astonishment.

'The man was riding up the hill to the city gates on a donkey. Behind him, children were vandalising olive trees in order to have branches to wave as the procession continued. The crowd ripped off their cloaks and threw them in front of the donkey in the manner usually associated with a coronation. Tension mounted at the entrance to Jerusalem where everyone except visiting kings, dismounts and walks into Jerusalem on foot. With a face set joyfully and yet determined, Jesus continued to ride the donkey straight through the gates. Tumultuous cheering followed.

'Swept away with enthusiasm, the market-stall holders pulled the wrapping from the parcels of dates they were selling and ran to join the crowd, waving the palm leaves as they went. Seconds later Jesus found himself at the centre of a violent disruption in the Temple. Here is a location report.'

**Interviewer's voice:** I have here a woman who is one of the many Jews who regularly worships God at the Temple.
**Woman's voice:** But never like this before, I can tell you!
**Interviewer's voice:** What do you mean?
**Woman's voice:** I've never seen such a commotion. The leaders were furious anyway, because people had been shouting, 'God bless the king, God bless the king'.
**Interviewer's voice:** To Jesus?

<50>

**Woman's voice:** Yes. And he loved it! The 'king of the Jews' they are calling him. He strode right past me in the Temple and started turning over the furniture.

**Interviewer's voice:** There was a riot?

**Woman's voice:** No, not a riot! He was quite controlled about it. The merchants have their stalls there, selling animals for the sacrifice, changing money because they only accept Temple coins inside. Jesus sent them all flying!

**Interviewer's voice:** You must have been heartbroken.

**Woman's voice:** Heartbroken! I was delighted. Thieves and crooks they are! Overcharging! Taking advantage of people! It's about time someone taught them a lesson! It's the best thing that's happened in my lifetime!

**Interviewer's voice:** And how would you describe Jesus' mood?

**Woman's voice:** Well, on the outside he looked determined. But when I was near him, I could hear him muttering. Crying! He was saying, 'Poor, poor Jerusalem. If only you knew what was about to happen. If only you knew!'

**Interviewer's voice:** And what do you think is about to happen?

**Woman's voice:** Trouble! I'm sure of it. Look! Look behind you! Here he comes again. My hero. God bless you, Jesus. Glory to God! Glory to God! God bless the king! God bless...

**Interviewer's voice:** Excuse me, could you ... could you ...? She seems to have gone. From the Temple in Jerusalem back to the studio.

'It is becoming clear that not everyone is as happy about Jesus' actions as his followers are. While those who have had their sins forgiven by him are rejoicing and changing their lives, others are complaining. In particular, Jewish leaders are trying to persuade people that Jesus is not who he says he is.

'Children played an important part in today's proceedings when they ran through the Temple entrance shouting, 'Glory to the one God has sent us.' Outraged that children should be making such a noise in praise of Jesus, nearby adults told Jesus to insist they be quiet. He refused to do so, suggesting that the children had a better idea how to praise him than the adults. Religious leaders left in great anger.

'Anne O'Pinion, let me bring you in at this point. Someone who God has sent to be king! That's what they seem to be saying about Jesus. Not possible, surely?'

*(Anne O'Pinion's reply should indicate that Jesus is a king, although not in the sense of a human monarch. He is someone to be praised and obeyed.)*

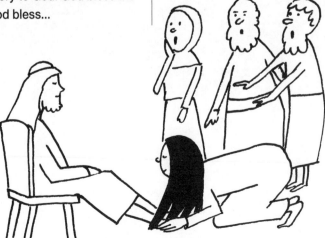

'What do you make of the incident in the Temple? People have gone there for centuries to worship God. If he doesn't want us to go to the Temple any more, what does he want us to do in order to please God?'

*(Anne's reply should explain something of what it means to live as a Christian day to day.)*

'Jesus seems to have a better attitude to children than the leaders in Jerusalem, but surely he is not expecting children themselves to become his followers, is he?'

*(Anne's reply should show that anyone is able to follow Jesus, no matter how young, and that he loves to welcome people as his friends.)*

<51>

'Thank you, Anne. And from the two of us in Studio 2, back to the *Newshounds* show.'

## 10.55 <7.10>
### The Daily Hound

The children go to their groups for today's newspaper.

## 11.15 <7.30>
### Gladihound

Today's round of the game show. The subject for the list is ... television soap operas.

## 11.30 <7.45>
### Houndaround

Another interview with one of the leaders.

## 11.40 <7.55>
### The Really Kicking Hound Show

Repeat songs that have been learnt in the last few days. If a new one is to be learnt today, the following are appropriate:

- The *Newshounds* song
- King of kings and Lord of lords
- Let's talk about Jesus
- Joy is the flag flown high
- Jesus rode a donkey into town
- Jesus put this song into our hearts

(Songs can be found in the *Junior Praise* and *Praise God Together* songbooks.) At some point during the singing introduce a chant of praise to Jesus. Establish a rhythm by clicking fingers, then say the words, 'Praise to Jesus, King of kings, his love goes on for ever more'. The finger click comes on alternate beats (praise, Je-, King, kings, love, on, ev-, more). Repeat it four times, starting very quietly and getting louder each time.

Ask children to think: 'If a king came into the room this moment, what would be the right thing to do?' After a few seconds to think, ask for some suggestions (eg, bow to him, obey him, greet him, cheer him). As ideas are suggested, make a list of them. The leader should then say a prayer to Jesus the King, incorporating all the ideas that children have offered.

## 11.55 <8.10>
## Studio dialogue

**Producer:** (*Coming in and interrupting.*) See you in the morning. Whoops! Sorry!

**Link man:** And now our late night movie. And for all you old time movie buffs, here's the classic favourite, *The Hound of the Newservilles*. Hi (*name*). I don't know who writes this trash.

**Producer:** I think I've got a pretty good idea.

**Link man:** You know two people out of every three in Judea listened to your broadcast tonight. There's more interest in Jesus than there is in the Rome Olympic games.

**Producer:** Story like this! I can't lose.

**Link man:** And neither can Jesus.

**Producer:** Oh boy, yes he can. Jake Newshound broadcast the facts tonight. He didn't broadcast the rumours.

**Link man:** Rumours?

**Producer:** Death threats. Secret deals with assassins. Behind the scenes betrayals.

**Link man:** Is this for real?

**Producer:** I can't bear it (*name*), I really can't. He's a lovely man, a lovely, lovely man. And he's heading for...

**Link man:** Isn't there anything you can do? With the audience you've got for Jake's show, you could have a big influence.

**Producer:** We're there to report the news, not make it. Your red light is flashing.

**Link man:** Commercials coming up. Got to go. See you tomorrow.

**Producer:** Bye.

## 12.00 <8.15>
## Closedown

The overall coordinator brings the meeting to a close and says goodbye to the children.

# Newshounds DAY 4

**STUDIO REPORT** Luke 22:7–23:56 (John 16:16-19; 19:30)

Having foreseen his death, Jesus is arrested in an olive plantation, tried before an illegal court, condemned to death and executed.

**NEWSPAPER REPORT** Luke 5:17-26

As a paralysed man discovered, through Jesus we can have our sins forgiven.

## 9.30 <6.15>
### Leaders' preparation

Thank God that he loves to forgive people and ask that this may be a day when he will take joy in forgiving many adults and children. Then read Luke 5:17-26 and 23:26-46, and discuss some or all of these questions:

**1** Who in Luke 5:17-26 do you find yourself identifying with, and why?

**2** If the paralysed man was forgiven without saying a word, could it be that some children can be forgiven by Jesus without saying a word? Or should we ask them to say a particular prayer and follow a set formula?

**3** How do you anticipate that the children will react to the heartbreaking and emotional story of Jesus' crucifixion, especially if they are hearing it for the first time? How should you be ready to respond to these reactions?

Hold a silence in which individual leaders can speak to God about their own need for forgiveness, then suggest that each leader reads the names of all the children in his or her group, asking for Jesus' love to captivate them.

## 10.15 <6.30>
### Opening credits

Welcome and register children, showing any new children to their groups. On today's press pass, children should draw and colour something that represents their favourite films and programmes on television.

## 10.30 <6.45>
### Headlines

The children gather, the jingle plays at an exciting volume and the presentation begins:

**Link man:** The time is (*correct time*). The date is (*today's date*). The place is the *Newshounds* holiday club. This is the news!

<53>

# PRESS PASS
## IDENTITY

*Event*
**Newshounds**

*Day*
**Four**

*Name*

These are my favourite films and TV shows

A new report out today on the state of public transport has revealed the shock statistic that only one in ten buses are running on time. The rest are running on wheels.

A group of local cats have released the information that they are going to start up a rival to *The Daily Hound*. It is going to be called *The Mews-paper*.

Sports news! A big shock today for Cinderella. It has been announced that she has been dropped from the national football team. The manager said, 'We're disappointed in her performance lately. She keeps running away from the ball.'

*(Other localised news-jokes can be added.)*

And now for news of today's *Newshounds* show, here is (*name of the overall coordinator*).

The co-ordinator welcomes the children and announces any notices that need to be given.

## 10.35 <6.50>
## Studio dialogue

**Link man:** I am (*name*). That was the news. And now the long-running school drama, *Grange Hound*.
**Producer:** (*Entering anxiously*.) Have you heard anything?
**Link man:** Oh hi, (*name*)! You're really on edge, aren't you?
**Producer:** So have you heard anything?
**Link man:** I've never known a news story get to you like this.
**Producer:** It's not just a news story. It's … It's … Don't you see, my whole life's wrapped up in this?!
**Link man:** You think there might be a promotion in it?

**Producer:** Garbage a promotion. I'm talking about life. I'm talking about something … something worth dying for.
**Link man:** Wow! You're serious. You're a changed man, you know.
**Producer:** So have you heard anything? Please!
**Link man:** I'm not supposed to say. It's all unconfirmed rumours and sightings.
**Producer:** Please, (*name*)… (*Name*), please…
**Link man:** Apparently he's gone to a garden. On the south side of the Mount of Olives. He's…
**Producer:** Thanks. Bye! (*Rushes away*.)
**Link man:** (*Name*), it's dangerous… (*Name*), be careful… I worry about you. Dear God, I worry about him… What! … Oh yes, of course, on with the show.

## 10.40 <6.55>
## Aerobihound

The link man ad libs: 'And now, with arms like armour, with muscles like missiles, with legs like logs, and brains like a brick, here she is, the fine-fingered, ten-toed, knobbly-kneed marvel, (*name*).'

## 10.45 <7.00>
## *Newshounds—Location Report* video or *Good News at Ten* drama

If the video is being used, show episode four. If the broadcasts are being performed live, play the introductory music that announces Jake Newshound, Anne O'Pinion, and the pre-recorded 'eye-witness' interview:

'*Good News at Ten*. This is Jake Newshound reporting on the Jesus phenomenon.

'A day of disappointment for those who have been following Jesus. Last night he was reported to be having a meal in private with his closest followers. Sources close to Jesus said that he stressed the importance of those who love him remembering him. In words that now suggest an uncanny foresight into what was

to come, he told his friends, "In a little while you will see me no more." Mysteriously he added, "And then you will see me again."

'The small group made their way to an olive farm on the side of a hill known locally as the Mount of Olives. Jesus at this point moved out of sight with his three closest associates. It is believed that he went to pray to God for strength, but the exact nature of this cannot be ascertained since the rest of his followers were asleep.

'A short time later there were alarming noises. A crowd had come carrying flaming torches and home-made weapons of all sorts. The mood seemed to be very angry indeed. Astonishingly, among the crowd were people who had been cheering him into Jerusalem at the beginning of the week. It became obvious that their leaders had a warrant to arrest Jesus. It is indeed incredible that his popularity has turned so completely to hatred in such a short time. This report was filed shortly after the events.'

<54>

**Interviewer's voice:** Can you explain what you saw here in this garden?

**Man's voice:** A huge crowd came for Jesus. Soldiers. Religious leaders. Thugs. They looked full of rage. I went and hid.

**Interviewer's voice:** Did Jesus hide too?

**Man's voice:** No, he just let them come. Then one of his friends came up and greeted him. That must have been a sign they had arranged because, as soon as they saw that, the soldiers surged forward to grab him.

**Interviewer's voice:** Did I hear you right? One of Jesus' own friends has been responsible for having him arrested?

**Man's voice:** Yes, a man named Judas. I can hardly believe it myself. It's hideous. Hideous!

**Interviewer's voice:** Are you trying to tell me that no one did anything to protect him?

**Man's voice:** Oh they tried to. Some of Jesus friends had swords and were obviously ready to fight back. One of them struck out, but Jesus told them to put their swords away.

**Interviewer's voice:** How would you say the great man sounded?

**Man's voice:** This sounds strange, but it was as though he was expecting them. He seemed quite calm. You know, it was as if *he* was in control of the situation, not the mob.

**Interviewer's voice:** What did he say?

**Man's voice:** I heard him say, 'This is the hour when the power of darkness rules.' And then they dragged him away. It's awful. It's the worst day of my life.

**Interviewer's voice:** And his followers. Where are they?

**Man's voice:** Run away. All of them. Like terrified mice. Left him all alone. Whatever will happen to him now?

**Interviewer's voice:** So you think this is the end?

**Man's voice:** No. It can't be. Whatever happens now, it can't be the end. I'm just too scared to know what to do for the best.

**Interviewer's voice:** We wish you well on this grim night. And now back to the studio.

'A great deal has happened in the hours since then. Jesus was taken to a session of the Jewish court. It is the first time the court has met by night – something previously held to be illegal. From there Jesus has been taken from one prison to another in a series of appearances before Roman judges and authorities. The bruising and bloodstains suggest that at each stage he was viciously beaten by prison guards. On no occasion was there any sign of resistance by Jesus, nor a word of complaint.

'The crowd has been growing increasingly murderous all night. At one point they were yelling for his death. Then after a dawn meeting with the Roman governor, sentence of execution was passed. Jesus was led from the prison dragging a wooden beam on his shoulders. At the execution site the soldiers nailed his hands to the beam, which was then hauled up a tree and attached to its branches. Amid jeering and taunts from a hateful crowd he hung on the cross until he ... excuse me ... until he died of exhaustion.

'Anne O'Pinion, a heartbreaking day for you. Thank you for agreeing to be here in these circumstances. Much here that is hard to understand. "It is finished." His last words. More a shout of triumph than of failure. What could he have meant?'

*(Anne O'Pinion's reply should explain that Jesus knew he was going to be killed and that it was part of his plan to bring humans back to a friendship with God.)*

'And those other words, "Father, forgive them. They don't know what they are doing". Why should a man in those awful circumstances say that?'

*(Anne's reply should show Jesus to be unlike any other, full of love and compassion, even for those who were harming him.)*

'That mysterious saying, "You will see me no more, but then you will see me again." What could that have meant?'

*(Anne's reply should foreshadow the resurrection, leaving children clear that the death of Jesus is not the end of the story.)*

'Anne, many of our viewers will want to believe you, but of course, as we all know, it is impossible for an ordinary man to return to life. Why, only God himself has that sort of power! From a studio sick at heart at today's events, goodnight.'

## 10.55 <7.10>
## The Daily Hound

The children go to their groups for today's newspaper. It may be necessary for leaders to be aware that children who do not know about the resurrection may be distressed at the story of the crucifixion, so it is quite appropriate for leaders to explain what the children will hear in tomorrow's club – that Jesus rose from the dead and will never die again.

There is also a possibility of a

<55>

slight confusion with the newspapers today, since the Bible story children have just heard is about his death, but the newspaper story shows him alive. It should be explained that the newspaper report is of an event earlier in Jesus' life, before his execution. (It is not by accident that the forgiveness of sins and the crucifixion are linked by having them both discussed on the same day: although, as far as the children are concerned, it is enough that the link is there; it does not need attention drawn to it.)

<56>

## 11.15 <7.30>
## Gladihound

Today's round of the game show. The subject for the list is ... people whom Jesus met.

## 11.30 <7.45>
## Houndaround

Another interview with one of the leaders.

## 11.40 <7.55>
## The Really Kicking Hound Show

Repeat songs that have been learnt in the last few days, adding a new one which reflects on the crucifixion:

• The *Newshounds* song
• I'm special because God has loved me
• God is so good
• My Lord loves me
• He made the stars to shine
• There is singing in the desert
• On Calvary's tree He died for me

(These songs can be found in the *Junior Praise* and *Praise God Together* songbooks.) At an appropriate moment during the songs, use this prayer of confession, the children responding to the leader with the repeated italic line:

The Lord Jesus longs for us to turn away from our sins so that he can forgive us, so we say:

For the actions which have angered you, we are truly sorry;
*Jesus, please forgive and help us.*
For the words which have wounded you, we are truly sorry;
*Jesus, please forgive and help us.*
For the thoughts which have betrayed you, we are truly sorry;
*Jesus, please forgive and help us.*
For the failures which have let you down, we are truly sorry;
*Jesus, please forgive and help us.*
Amen.

Remind the children that because of what Jesus has done on the cross the wrong things we have done can be completely forgiven. Say a prayer thanking Jesus for this. Invite the children to go round drawing a cross with their fingers on the palms of those close to them, saying each time, 'Jesus has forgiven us'.

## 11.55 <8.10>
## Studio dialogue

**Link man:** Well, at this point we were going to broadcast the next episode of the puppet drama, *Thunderhounds* but, in view of the news from Jerusalem, that seems inappropriate tonight. So instead we are going to play some sombre music. Here is the Galilee Symphony Orchestra. (*Long silence*). Well, it's over then.
**Producer:** I can't believe it finished like this.
**Link man:** All good men die young.

**Producer:** Yes, but without a fight? And his followers. Hundreds of them. Thousands of them. Melted away.
**Link man:** They're scared.
**Producer:** Of course they're scared. I'm scared!
**Link man:** What have you done?
**Producer:** Produced a show that gave news about him again and again in top-rating broadcasts. That's what I've done.
**Link man:** Can they jail you for that?
**Producer:** You know the Romans. They can jail you for sneezing in the presence of an army officer.
**Link man:** You've got to be strong. People who ran away will want to know what to do. They will be watching the broadcasts looking for hope.
**Producer:** I've got no hope to give them. All I can say is, it's all over. Now go to bed.
**Link man:** I don't think it's all over. There must be somewhere else to go.
**Producer:** There is. Sleep, like everyone else. The best week in my life has turned into the worst week in my life. I'm tired through.
**Link man:** Goodnight!
**Producer:** Goodn... No. Nothing's good any more.

## 12.00 <8.15>
## Closedown

The overall coordinator brings the meeting to a close, assures the children that today's episode is not the end of the story and says goodbye to them. If an all-age service is being held at the climax of the club, today is probably the best day to send home invitations for children to give to the adults with whom they live.

# Newshounds DAY 5

## STUDIO REPORT Luke 24:1-53

People claim to have seen Jesus alive again, until finally his appearance before a large group of his followers leaves them in no doubt and they mark Jesus' return to heaven as an occasion for great joy and determination about the future.

## NEWSPAPER REPORT Luke 19:1-9

As Zacchaeus found after meeting Jesus, following him makes a remarkable practical difference to the way we live our lives.

### 9.30 <6.15>
### Leaders' preparation

Pray that Jesus will become more real to and more fully understood by every adult and child in the club today. Then read Luke 19:1-9 and 24:36-53, and discuss some or all of these questions:

**1** When can you remember being 'filled with great joy' (Luke 24:52) at something to do with your faith in the risen Jesus? Share your recollection with the other leaders.

**2** Is there any kind of child who we tend to assume is, like Zacchaeus, impossibly unlikely to respond to Jesus?

**3** How do we know that Zacchaeus' change was genuine, and what can we learn about what Jesus looks for in his followers? Does he look for different things in children than he looks for in adults?

Pray that, in God's time and in God's way, the children at the club will become changed people. Pray for continued contact with children beyond this final day.

### 10.15 <6.30>
### Opening credits

Welcome and register children, who should by now be familiar with the routine of going to their groups. On today's press pass, children should draw and colour something that shows what their favourite part of the *Newshounds* holiday club has been.

### 10.30 <6.45>
### Headlines

The children gather, the jingle plays at an exciting volume and the presentation begins:

<57>

## PRESS PASS
### IDENTITY

*Event*
**Newshounds**

*Day*
**Five**

*Name*

These are my favourite parts
of Newshounds

<58>

**Link man:** The time is (*correct time*). The date is (*today's date*). The place is the *Newshounds* holiday club. This is the news!

Reports are coming in that a gang of robbers have broken into the local butcher and stolen a huge quantity of meat. Police have asked everyone to help their enquiries by keeping a look-out for a load of beef-burglars.

Tributes have been pouring in following the death of Harry the Hedgehog, star of TV show *The Harry Hedgehog Hour*. He was run over by a ten-ton tank while crossing the main road. One of his closest friends said, 'It is a terrible accident and I am heartbroken. He used to be my flatmate'.

And finally, some sports news. The manager of third division Manic United has just presented each of his team with a lighter. When asked why he did this, he said, 'It's because they keep losing their matches!'

*(Other localised news-jokes can be added.)*

And now for news of today's *Newshounds* show, here is (*name of the overall coordinator*)

The coordinator welcomes the children and announces any notices that need to be given.

## 10.35 <6.50>
### Studio dialogue

**Link man:** I am (*name*). That was the news. And now the weather, with the nation's favourite broadcaster, Jake Newshound. Are you there? ... Are you there in studio 2, Jake? Well, there seems to be a technical hitch there. We can't get the report for you at the moment, so we have some time in hand... It does seem to be

freshening up, doesn't it? I wouldn't be surprised if there's rain before the weekend's out. I wish I'd brought a cardigan with me now ... Still no sign of the weather forecast, but if I were you I'd be prepared for every possibility, rain or fine. As my grandmother used to say, you can never be too sure with the weather... Um... Um...

**Producer:** (*Rushing in at full tilt.*) He's alive.

**Link man:** Ah! Here's (*name*) to take over this delayed weather report.

**Producer:** I'm going.

**Link man:** You can't. You're on air.

**Producer:** You're on air. I'm on cloud nine.

**Link man:** I've told them you're doing the weather. Now!

**Producer:** Do it for me. Please! I'm gone!

**Link man:** You can't walk out on me now. You can't. You just can't.

**Producer:** Watch me!

**Link man:** But why?

**Producer:** There's word going round. Someone says someone's seen Jesus alive.

**Link man:** Don't be absurd.

**Producer:** Why not? Give me one good reason why I shouldn't be absurd.

**Link man:** Because it's impossible.

**Producer:** Of course it is! Do you think I'd walk out in the middle of a broadcast for something that's boringly possible?

**Link man:** Don't do this to me. It's inhuman.

**Producer:** You're too right it's inhuman. That's what I'm going to report. I've got to make a programme which shows that a human can't do this. He must be... He must be...

**Link man:** God!

**Producer:** He must be God. There's no other explanation. Keep talking. Fill in for me.

**Link man:** I must be mad!

**Producer:** You are! And I love you.

**Link man:** Since when?

**Producer:** Since five minutes ago when I first heard the rumour. I love you, I love him, I love... I love life.

**Link man:** It had better be true!

**Producer:** True? I'm staking my life on it.

**Link man:** I want witnesses. I want evidence. I want eye-witness accounts.

**Producer:** I want to see him again. I'm going. (*Exit.*)

**Link man:** Go, and God go with you. And God help me. And God, please let this be true.

## 10.40 6.55
### Aerobihound

The link man ad libs: 'And now, to lead Aerobi-hound for the final time this week, five-foot-five of fabulous, fine, physical fitness; the pride of the press ups, the joy of the joggers, the sport of the speedy and the run of the mill. For the last time, give it up for the magnificent (*name*).'

## 10.45 <7.00>
### Newshounds—Location Report video or Good News at Ten drama

If the video is being used, show episode five. If the broadcasts are being performed live, play the introductory music that announces Jake Newshound, Anne O'Pinion, and the pre-recorded 'eye-witness' interview:

'Good News at Ten. This is Jake Newshound reporting on the Jesus phenomenon.

'A quite unbelievable change has come over the supporters of Jesus in the past twenty-four hours. Meeting tonight at a secret location, his closest associates had locked the door for fear that the army would systematically eliminate all who have been involved in Jesus' work over the last three years. The atmosphere was said to be tense and desperately sad.

'I am told that early in the morning a knock representing their secret code was given. A group of women, breathless and in a state of excitement, came in. They broke the news that they had just been to the cave where Jesus body had been laid in order to embalm it with spices, as is the local practice. When they arrived, they discovered that Jesus' body was missing!

'Looking round in shock, they discovered that they were in the presence of two angelic characters who gave them a breathtaking message. It was this: "Jesus is not here. He has come back from life and is risen from the dead. Go and tell his followers to prepare to meet him." The women had run to bring this good news to the eleven men in the room and immediately left to spread their joy at this marvellous turn of events to others.

'As if this was not enough, further mind-blowing events were still to come. In this report from a location in Jerusalem, one of the eye-witnesses takes up the story.'

**Interviewer's voice:** I have with me one of Jesus' closest followers, who is almost breathless with excitement.
**Man's voice:** I've seen him. I've seen him!
**Interviewer's voice:** Can you explain what it is you saw?

**Man's voice:** I was in Jerusalem, meeting with the other followers. I could hardly believe what I was hearing. First, the women had told me they'd seen Jesus alive. Then Simon. Then Cleopas. I was beginning to think that I was the only person who hadn't seen Jesus since he rose from the dead. And then, there he was. In the room with us!
**Interviewer's voice:** How did he get in the room?
**Man's voice:** Don't ask me! He was just ... there! Standing among us.
**Interviewer's voice:** What did he say?
**Man's voice:** He said, 'Peace be with you.' It was the most beautiful message I've ever heard.
**Interviewer's voice:** And what did you say?
**Man's voice:** Absolutely nothing. I thought I was looking at a ghost. I was speechless.
**Interviewer's voice:** So it was a ghost, not a real man?
**Man's voice:** No, no, no! It couldn't be a ghost! He said he was hungry. Ghosts don't get hungry. We gave him the leftovers from our supper. It was only a bit of fish but ... well, we were overcome with joy, my hands weren't steady enough to go and cook a meal!
**Interviewer's voice:** And does Jesus look the same now as he always did?

**Man's voice:** Yes... No... Yes and no! He looks marvellous, completely glorious, not like someone who has just died. But he still has the scars in his hands and feet of where the nails held him to the cross. I guess he'll have those forever.
**Interviewer's voice:** Wonderful news! Thank you, and back to the studio.

'Some time later, Jesus was reported to have gone to Bethany. While there, he gave his friends instructions to keep on following him even when they could not see him any more. He gave them the task of taking the good news that he is alive, and that lives are changed through him, as far as they can through the world. In a moment of great seriousness as well as joy, Jesus gave them his blessing.

'While his followers were taken up in prayer to God and praise of Jesus whom we must now, without doubt, refer to as the Son of God, Jesus returned to heaven. As far as we are aware, the followers have now returned to Jerusalem, where they are waiting in joyful anticipation that power will be given to them to do everything that Jesus has asked them to do. When asked whether he missed Jesus, one was quoted as saying, "How can I miss him? He has promised us that he will

<59>

still be with us wherever we go, as far as the very ends of the earth. I love him and feel so close to him, it is almost as if he were right inside me."

'Anne O'Pinion, I hardly know how to introduce you on this glorious occasion. Many of our listeners have been commenting on the fact that last night you seemed to have a strange insight that something as remarkable as this was going to happen. You mentioned that you felt there might be a plan in all this. Can you explain what you feel the plan was?'

*(Anne O'Pinion's reply should indicate that Jesus had said many times during his last three years that he would die and rise again. It was the only way that humans could have their sins forgiven and be restored to God as friends.)*

'You have made it quite plain to us that you believe that Jesus was God himself on earth and you are one of his followers. What has made you so sure?'

*(Anne's reply should explain to the children very briefly that being a Christian involves making your mind up so that, as a result of what you know about Jesus, you want to follow him.)*

'Before he returned to heaven, Jesus has told his friends to go on following him. It is easy to understand how people can be his friends while he is with them. But how can they follow him now that they can't even see him?'

*(Anne's reply should be about what it means in practical terms to live a Christian life.)*

'After these events it seems that none of us can think in the same way about death again. Is this the end of death as we know it?'

*(The reply should explain that, because of what Jesus has done, his followers too will live in heaven for ever in complete joy.)*

'Thank you. From Anne O'Pinion and me, in an overjoyed Studio 2, back to the *Newshounds* show.'

## 10.55 <7.10>
### The Daily Hound
The children go to their groups for today's newspaper.

## 11.15 <7.30>
### Gladihound

Today's round of the game show. The subject for the list is … cartoon characters.

## 11.30 <7.45>
### Houndaround

Another interview with one of the leaders.

## 11.40 <7.55>
### The Really Kicking Hound Show

Allow children to choose their favourite songs from the week. A new song which affirms today's teaching could be chosen from among the following:

• The *Newshounds* song
• He is Lord, He is Lord
• Christ is risen, hallelujah, hallelujah!
• Jesus Christ is risen today
• Sing and rejoice
• Be bold, be strong
• Zacchaeus was a very little man
• Jesus send me the Helper

(Most songs can be found in the *Junior Praise* and *Praise God Together* songbooks.) As a statement of what Christians believe, teach children this age-old statement and the hand actions that go with it:

Christ has died, (*Stretch arms wide in the shape of a cross.*)
Christ is risen, (*Hold arms in front of you at chest level.*)
Christ will come again, (*Point upwards.*)

Having learnt it, say it together after each of these lines spoken by the leader and corresponding to each of the five days' teaching:

We believe that Jesus loves and cares for every person in the world…
We believe that Jesus has all the power and glory of God himself…
We believe that Jesus is King and wants us to follow him…
We believe that Jesus died on the cross so our sins can be forgiven…
We believe that Jesus came alive and lives for ever more…

Hold a time of thanksgiving. Ask the children to think for a few moments: 'If Jesus was in the room right now and you had a chance to say thank you to him, what is the thing you would most like to thank him for?' Invite them to tell the person sitting next to them what they have decided on. Give them about fifteen seconds to do this.

Then hold a time of open prayer, suggesting that any child who wishes to says, 'Thank you, Jesus, for…' *(whatever he or she has decided on)*. Stress that if two people accidentally say their prayers at the same time it does not matter, because now that Jesus has risen from the dead and returned to heaven he can hear everyone at the same time.

<60>

The leader should say the first and last prayers to establish the structure and say a loud 'Amen' after each child's contribution as a mark of affirmation.

## 11.55 <8.10>
## Studio dialogue

**Link man:** So it was true?

**Producer:** So it was true!

**Link man:** You've got the scoop of the year.

**Producer:** I've got the scoop of a lifetime!

**Link man:** I hear you've been offered a promotion.

**Producer:** Yeah!

**Link man:** And the *Bad Times* have offered to make you Editor.

**Producer:** Yeah!

**Link man:** And you've had offers from the international news agencies set to make you a millionaire.

**Producer:** Yeah!

**Link man:** Lucky geezer! So, what have you decided to do?

**Producer:** Resign.

**Link man:** Resign?

**Producer:** Yeah!

**Link man:** Why?

**Producer:** I've decided to change my lifestyle.

**Link man:** Jesus?

**Producer:** Yeah!

**Link man:** You've decided to follow him?

**Producer:** Yeah!

**Link man:** You'll be broke!

**Producer:** Yeah!

**Link man:** You'll be in continuous danger!

**Producer:** Yeah!

**Link man:** You'll have as many people hate you as love you!

**Producer:** Yeah!

**Link man:** (*Pause.*) I reckon you'll be deliriously joyful.

**Producer:** (*Pause.*) Yeah!

**Link man:** What do you do when you've discovered the truth, and it gives your life a completely new meaning, and you know it won't end for the whole of eternity?

**Producer:** You thank God, you shake yourself into action, and you get out there and devote the rest of your life to it.

**Link man:** (*Long pause.*) Can I come with you?

**Producer:** Yeah!

**Link man:** Where are we going?

**Producer:** Where he sends us.

**Link man:** What are we going to do when we get there?

**Producer:** What he tells us.

**Link man:** This is good news, isn't it?

**Producer:** It's the best news.

**Link man:** Are you ready to follow?

**Producer:** Yeah!

**Link man:** Yeah! (*They put their arms round each others' shoulders and wander slowly away.*)

## 12.00 <8.15>
## Closedown

The overall coordinator brings the meeting to a close and says goodbye to the children. They need a reminder of date and time of the all-age service before they go.

<61>

<62>

# Newshounds
# ALL-AGE SERVICE

**NEWSPAPER REPORT** Colossians 1:3-6

'Everywhere in the world that Good News is bringing blessings and is growing.'

## Setting

Although the service may take place in a different room, try to preserve some of the joyful atmosphere of the holiday club by transferring any decorations and craft for all to see. If there is a pulpit, it could be 'giftwrapped' in newspaper and flower displays could make imaginative use of newspaper as well. Copies of *The Daily Hound* could be displayed on the walls. Children should be encouraged to wear their press passes from the club and the service should prominently involve the adults whom the children have come to know.

If it is desired to distribute a final edition of the newspaper, it may be more appropriate to make this one an A4 version. Page 64 could be photocopied for every adult and child to have one, and a localised back page could be added in the usual way. Even the words of songs and the church notices could be presented in this way. It should be distributed as people arrive in the room.

## Welcome and hymn

The leader should greet the congregation in a way that makes them feel comfortable with the slightly unusual setting. Sing a hymn which may be familiar even to visitors but which is accessible to as many children as possible.

## Prayer

Everyone responds to the leader with the words in italics:

God has called us here this morning,
*All the world give God your praises.*
Let us offer him our worship,
*All the world give God your praises.*
Let us thank him for his goodness,
*All the world give God your praises.*
Let us ask him to forgive us,
*All the world give God your praises.*
Let us learn what he would teach us,
*All the world give God your praises.*
Let us bring our prayers before him,
*All the world give God your praises.*

Sing a new song to the Lord,
*He has done wonderful things.*

## Song

A leader who has been involved during the week should explain a little about what has happened, and then lead the *Newshounds* song.

## Bible reading

Another leader should read Colossians 1:3-6, having pointed out that everyone can follow the reading on their newspaper.

## Songs

Choose a selection of songs from those that have been used during the week.

## Prayers

Make the national newspapers of the past few days the basis for prayer. Different leaders, or older children who have been to the club, should read out headlines from the papers. (You could perhaps photocopy headlines and photographs onto acetate so that they can be displayed on an overhead projector during the prayers.) First of all focus on events in the world which show the damage that sin can do, and base a prayer of confession on those events. Then read out some items of good news and respond to them with thanksgiving. Finally, draw attention to people and places in the world where there is great need, and offer prayers of intercession for them.

## Song

Sing one of the more substantial songs from those used during the holiday club.

## Talk

The talk is based on the names of four newspapers, and a copy of each of them should be displayed as a visual aid.

### • THE NEWS OF THE WORLD

Why is it that the papers are so full of bad news? Because the world is full of good things and bad things together, but unfortunately people like reading about the bad things more than the good. It is because there is so much wrong in the world that Jesus came into it, for only he can forgive what is wrong and give people a new friendship with God. And, unlike some of the news in the papers, that is a true message (Colossians 1:5b).

### • THE SUN

Just as the sun lights up the world our lives can be transformed by Jesus. With him as a friend we have someone to pray to about all the good and bad in our lives, knowing that his love for us never falters for a moment, and someone whose example will show us how to care for each other in a way we never thought possible (1:3-4).

### • THE GUARDIAN

Jesus wants the very best for us. He will continually show us the right way to live in order to make the very best of our lives, and he will guide us all the way from here to the perfect safety and joy of heaven to come (1:5a).

### • THE DAILY HOUND

The holiday club newspaper has been a 'good news' newspaper. Just look at today's headline! It is true that the Good News about Jesus has been spreading for two thousand years now and has reached every part of the world (1:6). *Newshounds* has been part

of that, spreading the Good News among the children of the area. (*Take the opportunity to thank all those who have been part of the leadership team.*) So now you have heard this wonderful news about the friendship we can have with the living Jesus, who are you going to tell?

## Song

Bring the service toward its conclusion with an accessible hymn about following Jesus or the *Newshounds* song for a final time.

## Closing prayers

Among our children, who truly
    need Jesus,
*May the Good News keep on
    spreading.*
Among our teenagers, who truly
    need Jesus,
*May the Good News keep on
    spreading.*
Among our adults, who truly need
    Jesus,
*May the Good News keep on
    spreading.*
All round our church, which truly
    needs Jesus,
*May the Good News keep on
    spreading.*
Across our nation, which truly
    needs Jesus,
*May the Good News keep on
    spreading.*
Throughout our world, which truly
    needs Jesus,
*May the Good News keep on
    spreading.*

Christ, the Good News of all whose hope is set on him, bless you, guide you, and fill you with peace, this day and for ever more. Amen.

<63>

# The Daily Hound

**The Newshounds newspaper**

# Good news spreads worldwide

In the years after Jesus returned to heaven, our reporter Paul was one of those who took the Good News about him far and wide. And the best news is that there are more followers of Jesus in the world today than ever before in history.

IN OUR prayers for you we always thank God, the Father of our Lord Jesus Christ. We thank God because we have heard about the faith you have in Christ Jesus and the love you have for all of God's people.

## Hope for us all

You have this faith and love because of your hope, and what you hope for is saved for you in heaven. You learned about this hope when you heard the true teaching, the Good News that was told to you.

## Jesus brings blessings

Everywhere in the world the Good News is bringing blessings and is growing. This has happened with you, too, since you heard the Good News and understood the truth about the grace of God.

Reporter: Paul
Source: International Children's Bible
References: Colossians 1, verses 3 to 6

## THANKS!

The church wants to say a huge thank you to everyone who worked to make *Newshounds* holiday club a success. What better place to do it than in *The Daily Hound*! On behalf of all the children who had a happy time at the club, and their parents, thank you very much indeed.

## Puzzled?

There is definitely something missing from today's front cover picture. Join the dots to see one of Jesus' followers beginning to spread the good news about him.